*Deer Man Has the Antlers
to
Your Horny Questions*

The Best Of the "Outlanderish" Advice Column

*DEER MAN HAS THE ANTLERS
TO
YOUR HORNY QUESTIONS*

by

DEER MAN ANTLERS

illustrated by

Jeff Marlowe

T S PRESS
1226 Vine Ave., suite one
MARTINEZ, CALIFORNIA
1989

ISBN 0-9619375-8-0
Library of Congress Catalog Card # 89-90078

Printed in the United States of America
First Edition

Acknowledgments:

Judy Wright
Ralph Brown
Gaila Loring
Bons
Christina Singer
Linda Branscomb
Stephanie Jurs
Wilma Webster

DEDICATION

I got my thrill on Mary Jane Hill

ROLL OVER, ANN LANDERS!

We all know people who laugh at "dirty jokes." It's a fine old American tradition. Intelligent people with dirty minds are here in great supply. Yet how much amusing erotic literature is to be found? The (truly) tasteless joke books, and the ubiquitous intelligence-insulting hard core pornography represent about the only erotica available, leaving a veritable void in the marketplace.

As if that weren't bad enough, try the advice columns! A forum which could treat sex to such mirthful advantage, is currently dominated by goody two shoes twin sisters. The country's vast array of irreverent iconoclasts is left not with earthy belly laughs which should be their birthright, but sanctimonious sermonizing. And the only claim to humor is through the odd low class pun.

With the coming (as it were) of the incomparable, flamboyant, antler bedecked Deer Man Antlers, this situation is heroically reversed. Not only does he analyze sex in the clear light of his absurd perception of the world, but he vouchsafes myriad high class puns in the process. In addition, Deer Man offers purported poetry (in the form of sundry limericks and revisions of classic and folk poems) as well as quotes from and references to the gamut of art and wisdom over the entire history of civilization (to "broaden...readers' cultural horizons").

With evangelical flair, Deer Man elevates sex out of the gutter of porno shops and the know nothing tea parlors of dog-in-the-manger moral McCarthyites, exposing it to the light where weighty sexual concerns can be amusingly addressed. Note his crusade, for instance, to abolish the male-oriented sexual double standard which he says drives countless valuable women away from debauchery! Or join him in his gallant chagrin at "trigger-happy" men leaving women high and dry without even a decent shot at sexual release (Although, as Deer Man rightly observes, an indecent shot often obtains better results!).

Preaching the gospel of "Genteel Sex," Deer Man shows women how to "have orgasms like Grandma used to fake," and men how to avoid being a "phallus in blunderland." With refreshing candor and "self defecating" humor, Deer Man even confesses to his own anal fixations. No one and nothing is left out. Whether he is offering personal "Deer Manstrations," or "assisting" nymphomaniacs, "Deer Man cares."

Sometimes it is wise to keep a low profile. This book should probably be kept away from prying eyes. Deer Man is fond of the following quotation:

"It doesn't matter what you do, as long as you don't do it in public and frighten the horses."
—Mrs. Pat Campbell

GOOD JOB THE HORSES CAN'T READ!

DISCLAIMER

The people in this book do not exist (except in their own imaginations) and are professionals. Do not try these things at home.

Deer Man Antlers

I just broke up with my girlfriend. She had been pressuring me not to go to bed with her. I had resisted, not wanting to feel used. Well, she's stopped calling and I'm still just as horny, only now I'm without my girl. I wish I had been more of a goody goody instead of the lustful pervert I came across as. I am

Wet With Tears and Sticky Stuff

Dear Wet Behind the Tears

Don't speak slightingly of lustful perverts! That hits mighty close to home. Whatever you came across as, she didn't come across at all, which was the problem. Dry your tears. Your girlfriend was obviously only interested in one thing (not going to bed with you). If she really loved you, she would have waited and not gone to bed with you after you were married.

D.M.

Deer Man Antlers

I was at a Hallowe'en party (I'm 13). A girl there said she'd wanted to come as an angel, only she would've had to take her clothes off and she didn't know what to do for wings. I said I'd get behind her flapping my arms, which would serve as wings. But then she wanted to know how she could attach me to her. Do you have any suggestions? Write soon. I have a date in the pumpkin patch next Saturday. Until then I'll be

Winging It

Dear Pumpkin Patch Kid

She can probably come as an angel, or anything else, if you get behind her and are attached properly. This requires experienced adult supervision. Please send directions to the pumpkin patch. I will meet you there. Look for the nice man with antlers on his head.

D.M.

Deer Man Antlers

My girl and I had planned to be virgins when we got married. The other night we were drinking a lot. She passed out, and I was bored, so I took liberties with her. Is she still a virgin, since she was unconscious? I don't mind so much for myself, but I would feel bad for her. It was fun. If she's not, we might as well do it again, but I don't know how to break it to her. She still thinks she's

Pure As Driven Snow

Dear Snow Plow

Best thing is to marry her and put a little catsup discreetly on your thing. She'll think it was blood, and that it was her first time. If you don't want to marry her, whenever she does get married, tell her fiancé about this. He will be glad to do it for her. It's the least you can do. It would be too traumatic for her if you told her the truth. However, if she passes out again, there's no point in closing the barn door once the cow has escaped. Know what I mean?

D.M.

Deer Man Antlers

I'm a scientist with a bold hypothesis concerning where babies come from. I've done lots of experiments with promising results. What I believe is that babies come from screwing. I mean (in scientific parlance), sexual intercourse. I have seen so many of the women in my experiments swell up mysteriously shortly after I've personally subjected them to this procedure (which, I understand, isn't at all uncommon in the wild). Not, I believe, coincidentally, they deliver a baby exactly nine months later. Of course, though I've seen it happen time and time again, there have been numerous instances where it hasn't. That's the puzzling part. It seems to violate the first requirement of the scientific method, repeatability of the outcome of the experiment. But I intend to persevere at whatever sacrifice until I get 100% results, at which point I will propound what I call

The Big Bang Theory

Dear Science On a Wet Afternoon

Thanks for an inspiring letter. We're in a race with a time bomb (if you'll pardon a mixed metaphor). I refer of course to the population explosion. The person who discovers the secret of human reproduction will be a great hero. God bless and hang in there with your experiments.

D.M.

Deer Man Antlers

I have a huge nose, like Cyrano de Bergerac. I finally got off on my secret fantasy...You guessed it! The girl I tried it on thought I was being nosy but she didn't mind when my

Vorpal Schnozz Went Snicker Snot

YOUR HORNY QUESTIONS

Dear Blue Nose

What can I say? I just want to acknowledge that I learn so much from my readers. I thought I had heard it all! I guess for you, everything is coming up noses...

D.M.

Deer Man Antlers

I am a sincere pervert who would like some pointers. What I need to know is how to get more women to do weirder stuff. All I get now is a few conservative floozies who are only interested in the missionary position. Don't get me wrong—I've got nothing against missionaries! I'm a devout churchgoer myself. I think they just got a bad rap and in reality probably did it every which way. So where do the women who go for the strange stuff hang out? I can't seem to find any in church for some reason. Don't suggest some sleazy bar. I am a very

Particular Pervert

Dear Parishioner Pervert

This is a question that has been plaguing men through the ages. It ranks up there along with the search for the Fellatio stone and the Horny Grail. All I can say is, strange stuff is where you find it. I am, however, studying the possibility of bringing modern technology to bear on the problem. I am considering the creation of a central computerized Strange Stuff Hotline so that we can all have access to information concerning the whereabouts of these wonderful women. For now, though, let's use the Power of the Press to advantage. All you ladies out there who are into strange stuff, send me your phone numbers and an 8x10 glossy. Let's get the ball rolling.

D.M.

P.S. As a "devout churchgoer," I thought perhaps you would like an inspiring poem. Deer Man, incidentally, is a frustrated (yet first rated) poet. Good job he's got a column to use as a vehicle for artistic expression!:

> A girl of ecclesiastical bent
> Gave up going down, for Lent.
> She informed the town's men they
> Could still *fuck* her, but when they
> Went to church, they'd have to repent!

Deer Man Antlers

It's too late for me, but maybe it will save some of your readers from my fate if I tell you my story. Do you remember that song *Wake Up, Little Floozie?* Well, it happened to me. I was going out with a teenaged girl who was really hot for it. All I had to do was get her home by midnight (her mother thought she was babysitting for me).

Then one night we fell asleep. We didn't wake up until two in the morning. Of course, her mother won't let her "babysit" for me anymore. So now I'm reduced to watching dirty videos on the TV and it's

Masturbation City

Dear Television M.C.

Too bad you didn't have an alarm cock.

D.M.

Deer Man Antlers

Man antlers! Ha! That means you've got horns! That means somebody's screwing your wife! I bet it's me! Ha! Is she a looker? Send me one of your famous 8x10 glossies. I want to see if she's the one I'm screwing. I'm enclosing one of me so that you will despair.

The Other Man

"Nice nuptials!"

YOUR HORNY QUESTIONS

Dear Other Fucker

You sure know how to hurt a guy. But you're not so special. Every other man is screwing my wife. Let's face it, she's not very discriminating. Which would explain her screwing you, judging from your photo.

D.M.

Aside to readers—I'm just ribbing this guy. I don't really have a wife. Deer Man is what you call eligible with a capital E. All photos and phone numbers from cute *female* (homosexuals, please take note) readers will receive a response.

Confidential to So I'm All Wet! What Are You Going To Do About It?—I'm already in my fierce pajamas!

DEER MAN ANTLERS

Deer Man Antlers

I was arrested in the ladies room of a ritzy hotel last week. It's not that I wanted to be weird or do any perversions in there or frighten anybody. I just wanted to boldly go where no man has ever gone before! What do you think of that?

Twentieth Century Explorer

Dear Twenty Cent Explorer

Yes, that *is* the last frontier.

D.M.

Deer Man Antlers

My girlfriend and I usually do it in the...well, in the ass. So she won't get pregnant. Last month we were both really drunk. We got carried away, trying the real stuff. Well, sure enough, she missed her period! We were scared, but the doctor said it was an hysterical pregnancy. Isn't that hysterical?

Close, But No Cigar

Dear Cigar Butt

Speaking of cigars, why not *try* one next time? It's surefire. Never got anybody pregnant. I understand if she does her Kegel exercises, she'll even be able to smoke it—blow rings and stuff (I saw that in one of those Emmanuelle movies). Be the life of the party, and no risk of cancer! I know a lady who does it with cigarettes; smokes two packs a day. I've never heard of anyone getting cancer doing it that way. Of course, John Wayne would say "She ain't no lady," but he's dead. Lung cancer.

D.M.

Confidential to Playing Hard To Get—That's funny. I play to get hard.

Deer Man Antlers

I am a cop with a funny story to tell. In my town a pair of mugger-rapists were terrorizing women. They would jump them in isolated locales, one from the front, one from behind. Well, things were getting bad. There was a lot of heat on the police department to do something about it. So they sent me out as a decoy (I dressed up as a woman, frequenting dark alleys). Sure enough, they attacked me. They pulled up my skirt and were going to have at me when the one in front yelled, "Now you've done it, Joe! You've gone all the way through!" What do you think of that?

Fearless Fuzz Dick

Dear Alley Oops

It appears your dick *was* pretty fearless. In fact, it must have been ready for action. Well, whatever turns you on. Thanks for an amusing story. Readers! Don't hesitate to send Deer Man your funny stories. The raunchier (within the confines of good taste, of course) the better! God, I love raunchy stories.

D.M.

Confidential to Sex Is Sacred—Yes, but why wait until Sunday? You part time saints give me a pain!

YOUR HORNY QUESTIONS

Deer Man Antlers

I drove my girl up to a lovers lane place and then told her, "Fuck or walk!" She got out and started to walk. I drove up alongside and yelled, "Heavy petting or walk!" She kept on walking. I drove up again and said, "I chew your nipples, or you walk!" She kept right on walking. Finally, in desperation, I yelled, "A kiss or walk!" Then she gave me a kiss (not much of one) and got in and I drove her home like a gentleman. But now she won't see me again. I'm in way over my head. Can you tell me what I did wrong?

Phallus In Blunderland

Dear Phallustine

Women don't like that kind of pressure. Besides, they like to feel in charge of the fuck. It's this new women's lib thing. Next time go in *her* car and sure as my antlers are twisty, she'll tell *you* to "fuck or walk!" Then you've got to plead with her like Br'er Rabbit not to be thrown into the Briar Patch and finally whimper "okay" in a little tiny voice. That's what they like.

D.M.

DEER MAN ANTLERS

"What could I do, Dear?
She called me a flaming faggot!"

YOUR HORNY QUESTIONS

Deer Man Antlers

You straight chauvinist pig! Don't you know that homosexuality is as old as the hills? Listen. Socrates was a famous pederast; all the ancient Greeks were. Everyone with any education knows that. You and your "high class," "genteel sex!" Face it. You heteros have been outclassed by queers for years! We practically founded civilization. You know why things are getting rotten in the world? Why there's a population explosion? Why women can't go out at night? I'll tell you why. Heterosexuality! I just want to issue an appeal, a clarion call to mankind before it's too late. Let all who love men take up the cry:

"Oscar Mayer, Get Your Wiener
Out Of Barbara Ann's Buns!"

Dear Wiener

What kind of hot dog in the manger attitude is this?

D.M.

DEER MAN ANTLERS

Deer Man Antlers

Ever since I started reading your column, I've been close to finding a girl. I haven't found one yet, but I'm getting hot. It's really exciting! When I do finally get one, I'm going to dedicate her to you. My pants are

Off Already

Dear Awful Randy

No woman can resist that.

D.M.

Confidential to My Dad Can Lick Your Mom—This is true. We don't call her Mommy Deerest for nothing.

YOUR HORNY QUESTIONS

Deer Man Antlers

My name is Virginia. I am very upset. A girl isn't supposed to have to ask for sex. In our society, that's the boy's job! Well, I don't get any action (except for a weird Russian named Vronsky, who is kinkier than a garden hose. And *he* soon lost interest) unless I'm really aggressive. What's with these guys? It used to be a girl could just bat her eyelashes and she'd have several hands up her skirt. But if *I* want to get laid, I practically have to knock on doors asking if anyone wants to fuck! (Or go bananas, if you get my drift.) It's not that I'm not cute either. Enclosed is an 8x10 glossy to prove it. And *everybody* has my phone number (I posted it in all the restrooms). Why aren't I getting laid more? Is it the fluoridated drinking water or what? Maybe I'll just throw myself under a train. Then they'll wish they had fucked me more! Sometimes a person

Just Wants Her Share!

Dear Wants Is Not Enough or Banana Karenina

Yes, Virginia, there *are* horny men! I don't know where (or what) you've been hanging out. I am told by my panel of experts that according to the laws of physics, there is a theoretical possibility that all the air could suddenly rush to one corner of the room, creating a vacuum at the breakfast table. If that could happen to the breakfast nook, perhaps it could happen to the breakfast nookie. Just hold your breath and wait for it to pass. Because you are indeed cute (I perused your glossy). I would call you but you seem to have forgotten to give me your phone number. Incidentally, that's rather humiliating. Apparently everyone but Deer Man has your number. Or, more likely, the other way around. And he's the one who can't get in touch with you. Notice that even when you could have gotten laid (by Deer Man, yet!), something goes awry. Perhaps you are jinxed or accident prone. Though if you stay prone long enough, I should think someone would take the hint.

D.M.

P.S. At least you're getting *some* action. With a name like that, you're lucky it wasn't one of these self-fulfilling prophecies. Things could be worse. Sometimes it's good to realize that we are much better off than many others. It makes us grateful for what we do have. Toward that end, I am publishing a sad poem about a young girl (probably named Virginia, too) who fared so much worse than yourself:

> A fetching young willowy maid
> Having hitherto never been laid
> Picked a young man who turned out
> To be a bit burned out.
> So, sadly, a virgin she stayed.

Readers! Want to get laid Deer Man style? Send for Deer Man's booklet, *The Genteel Fuck, and How To Fuck It!*

Deer Man Antlers

I answered a personal ad where the man claimed that he loved to dance. I, too, love to dance so I thought we might be compatible. Well, I've seen him three times. The only dancing he's interested in is the horizontal cha-cha (he's got two left feet at that). I told him I wanted to get down and get funky but I think he may have misunderstood.

Dancing Fan

Dear Fan Dancer

Did you hear the one about the man who danced the fandangle? He had a fan in one hand and his dangle in the other. You can't get any funkier than that.

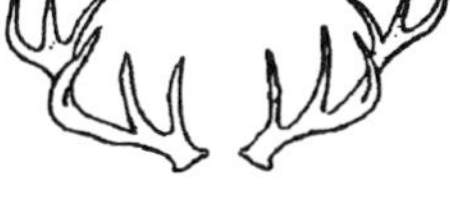

Deer Man Antlers

When I was hiking in the woods I heard muffled noises in the bushes. Creeping closer, I found a bunch of guys each waiting their turn to screw a naked girl. I had a camera so I took pictures, and followed her home from a discreet distance. I felt like Sam Spade or something. I discovered where the girl lives and have thought about showing these pictures to her mother unless she puts out for me too. Is this blackmail? What do you think about that?

Tempted Rat

Dear T. R.

Sneak softly and carry a big click, eh? Well, I can't give legal advice, but please send me *two* copies of these pictures and the girl's address.

D.M

Deer Man Antlers

Sex to me is very boring. Maybe I'm getting too much. All these women are coming on to me, then climbing off, leaving me in an advanced state of ennui. You will say I shouldn't be able to get it up if it's so boring, but I guess I must be a masochist that way. I'm not looking for sympathy. I just want you to know that some of us guys have it hard.

Bored Stiff

Dear B.S.

Guys like you give me a pain. With so many people going to bed horny at night, you ought to be ashamed to have such an ungrateful attitude. You should try to talk some of these women into taking a position as a mission-ary for the horny children in China. Or send me the par-ticulars (glossies and phone numbers). I will see that they get a chance to bestow their favors where I can personally assure you they will be appreciated.

D.M.

Confidential to Sex Was Just a Trick To Get Me Into Bed!—So what's wrong with trick *and* treat?

Deer Man Antlers

Isn't "Man Antlers" redundant? Did you ever hear of a lady with antlers? I mean a lady deer.

Deer Hunter

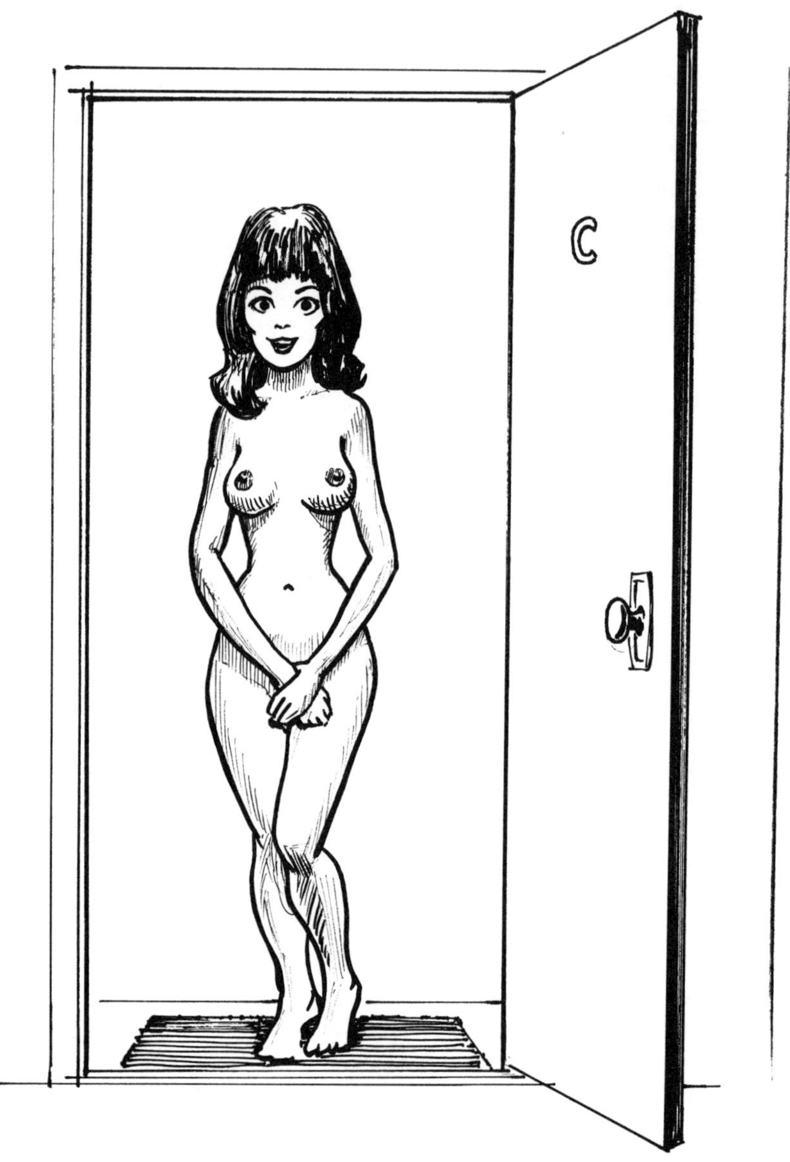

"I'm your third cousin, clothes removed..."

Dear Lady Killer

There *are* some horny women, and I want to take this opportunity to say I'd like to hear from them. Just be sure to enclose a photo (8x10 glossy will suffice) and your phone number.

D.M.

Deer Man Antlers

I am in therapy because I am afraid of sex. I am terrified of sex with men who are...well, too big. I'm even afraid of men who are too small (I'm worried they'll get lost in there). My psychiatrist says if I'm ever to get over my fear of "things that go hump in the night," I'll need to experience the sex in a safe, secure environment. He says his office would be perfect. I really trust him, so he'd be the ideal person to practise having sex with. Best of all, size is no problem. He says he can make himself bigger or smaller at will. But I understand his screwing me would be a breach of professional ethics. How can I keep him from losing his license? I don't want to kill the goose that eggs the

Golden Lay

DEER MAN ANTLERS

Dear Shrink To Fit

Just be sure to keep your mouth shut (except, of course, during therapy). When leaving his office, wipe away any shit-eating grin you may have on your face. It's a dead giveaway.

D.M.

Deer Man Antlers

I am hoping your antlers are more than hype. Do you really represent a fount of lore drawn from the rich heritage and wisdom of our American Indian traditions? If so, I request that you lay a weird Indian sex rite on your readers. Something with a virgin or a broom handle. Well, use your judgment. Whatever's at hand. Those are just some parameters. But make it raunchy, okay, horny guy?

Anthropology Buff

Dear Raunch Hand

Broom handles aren't actually Indian artifacts. Try witches. Now *they* had some weird rites, broomwise. It's sort of tame symbolism now, but you can imagine where the image of them riding around on brooms originated.

Indians were, however, big on virgins (I got big on one once, but that's another story). My favorite sex rite is where the elders of the tribe get to look at the wedding photographs (in Indian tradition, the photographer is allowed into the bridal chambers to record the consummation ceremonies). I also like the shots of the deflower girl doing her thing.

D.M

Confidential to She Strips and I Poke Her—Your letter (and your lady) inspired me to write a panegyric which should glorify fun loving women everywhere:

> A lady who was a real trouper
> Played strip poker and lost, which was super!
> For when she was nude,
> Her suggestions were lewd:
> She averred *she* was no party pooper!

Deer Man Antlers

There is something funny going on where I work. One of the stenographers is so cute it makes sick. She is always kissing up to the boss. I think she screws him on the floor in his office. I would like to screw him but he won't give me the time of day because I am plain. I thought of slipping some aphrodisiac pills into the coffee I bring him in the morning but it would probably be like those imprinted ducks that go for the first thing that moves, and this stenographer's got all the moves! I won't bother sending you a glossy but I just wonder if you've got any advice for an average looking girl (I'm not ugly at least) who isn't getting any action?

Jane In Plains

Dear Carter's Little Lover Pills or Georgia On My Mind

There's a fine organization you should try. It's called Perverts Without Partners. Anyone with lust in his heart can join. Please let me know if you get any. I would like a blow by blow account replete with spicy details. I care.

D.M.

Deer Man Antlers

You go on and on about "genteel" sex, but it is all heterosexual. You don't talk at all about high class homosexuality. But it's okay. I'm not big on sex manuals anyway. I like spontaneity, not something spelled out by a self-styled expert. You probably will make some lousy joke about my "guy by night" sexual orientation (I know you disdain homosexuals). But I just want to protest your sex-by-numbers formula approach. I prefer to fly by the seat of my pants. I am

An Artiste

Dear Anal Artiste

That was good about the "guy by night" thing. I wish I'd written it. You've got me eating my heart out. Which is still preferable to what you guys eat. About your fly by the seat of your pants—most people prefer theirs in front, but I understand some of you guys find it handier back there.

D.M.

P.S. For your information, I don't have anything personally against you guys. It's just that the stuff you're into seems awfully disgusting. Especially the kissing part. Guys kissing guys! Épouvantable!

DEER MAN ANTLERS

Deer Man Antlers

I've got a really swinging English teacher who would invite me to her house to help me with my lessons. I was getting really good at grammar and fucking, but then she got a boyfriend. Now she says I can't come anymore. What do you think of that? Now I'm left with

A Dangling Participle

Dear England Swings

Better to have fucked and lost than to have been told early on to fuck off. Have you offered to put a little English on it?

D.M.

Deer Man Antlers

Hello. My name is Lulu. They call me like, "Little Lulu" because I am so very petite and also...well, you know...because I also am so totally small where you...you know what. Anyway, I'd be fully stoked if you'd make me one of your ladies. I think it is a mistake for you to just go and, you know, *do* that with strange women. You could get majorly diseased. But I figure if you're going to make a mistake, you might as well make a, you know, Lulu.

YOUR HORNY QUESTIONS

I am enclosing my phone number and a glossy of me like on a bearskin rug. I'm not as young as I look (I promise—I'll show you my I.D. so don't worry). I just *look* like a Shirley Temple—without the cherry, of course. Sorry about that. Maybe I'll tell you how I, you know, lost it (at a totally gnarly party). I like, hear you enjoy dirty stories and I want to give you an extra incentive. This one is like, totally awesome. In fact, it's a lulu. That's my name—don't wear it out. Betcha can't wear me out! We'll make it the full contest, okay?

Lulu

Dear Lulu Of the Valley

Lay on Macduff. And damned be she who first cries "Hold! Enough!"

D.M.

Deer Man Antlers

I'm not a big fan of yours (I'm quite a petite lady). But would you elaborate on what you mean by "genteel" sex? I don't want to put on airs while getting laid. But I do want to have a class act. I am

Clay In Your Hands

DEER MAN ANTLERS

Dear Clay d'Oeuvre

Wonderful! My analyst loves me to get my hands in the fecal material. It's good therapy for my anal fixations (her specialty—I think that's why she's called that). But, seriously, to your question. Don't rush into it like hogs getting slopped. That is the main thing. No wham bam thank you ma'am quickies. It's like, when you go to a high class restaurant, you should take your time, savoring each course, soaking up the atmosphere and allowing the ambiance to have its way with you. The English are classy in this regard (too bad their food is the pits). I've spent many a pleasant afternoon in London having strumpets and tea (they call it high tea when strumpets are included).

Everything is a microcosm of the universe. So, during sex, you should meditate on the "holeness" of things. And when you come, may it be with the force of a thousand suns exploding (old Indian proverb)!

It all boils down to the origin of the universe, whether you subscribe to the Big Bang Theory or the Pig Bang Theory. That's what separates the wheat from the chaff.

Send me an 8x10 glossy of yourself and your phone number. Perhaps we can arrange a "Deer Manstration."

D.M.

DEER MAN ANTLERS

Deer Man Antlers

Your column could be a valuable service, giving advice to people who can't get it up or who are having serious sex problems. Instead, you use it as a vehicle for dumb jokes and pornographic titillation. I have such a problem, but I won't tell you about it because you'd just make fun of my

Bippie Balls

Dear BBs

Now, let's get this straight. You fuck with your pecker, see, not with your balls. I guarantee if you get up a hefty member nobody is going to notice your diminutive balls. Perhaps though, you've got a bippie shlong to go along with your bippie balls, in which case I can't help you (but I promise not to laugh).

D.M.

P.S. If it would make you feel better to know you aren't alone, I will publish my little inspiring poem about a lady with a corresponding size problem and how *she* solved it:

A frustrated virgin whose hole
Was as small as the eye of a mole
Dressed up as a man
And offered her can
To a sodomite out on a stroll.

Confidential to I Want To Ball *Now!*—Have patience, dear. Cleopatra wasn't fucked in a day. (It took Caesar's army six days and seven nights, I believe.)

Deer Man Antlers

Do you go out in public with your antlers on? Don't you feel ridiculous? I can't think of anything more absurd than a grown man with horns on his head. You call that sexy? I'll show you sexy. Enclosed is an 8x10 glossy of a real deer. I mean a wild stag. Not this pseudo-stud routine of yours. I used to settle for a man, but since I've discovered my animal instincts, I have reverted to

Animal Husbandry

DEER MAN ANTLERS

Dear Revert Prevert

You don't even say what sex you are. I think you're one of those homosexuals who found even that abomination too tame for your kinky tastes. Pretty soon you'll be dressing your wild stag up in ladies' clothes and buggering him with a broom handle.

D.M.

Deer Man Antlers

Whatever happened to the old fashioned virtues? Like honesty in packaging? At a restaurant you have a choice of "large, medium, or small," when accuracy would have been served by the labels "small, dinky, and microscopic." Or at the porno theaters they advertise that the girls will perform "sex acts." Well, I ask you, is a naked girl with a teddy bear a "sex act?" What is the world coming to? In the old days, honesty and truth in advertising were powerful values. Grandma was prone to exaggeration, but never once did she take off her clothes, hug my teddy bear, and call it a "sex act" (she always said it was "playing with dolls"). 'Course, we all had fun with Teddy. Even now, as I think of the little furry tyke, I get a lump in my throat (and somewhere else). Maybe it's honest advertising after all.

Never Mind

Dear Fuckraker

We all have our acts to grind. See next letter for a kindred spirit!

D.M.

Deer Man Antlers

My girl just won't put out. You can lead a horse to water, but how can you make it bend over? Don't tell me to find another horse, because you haven't seen her. And anyway, this is a one horse town. Just looking at her makes me so hot I'm practically smoking. Are there any Indian magic spells, mystical yogi incantations, or a just plain sex hex I can use on her? It's such a waste, too, because when it comes to sex, I'm loaded for bear. I've threatened to move and she doesn't

Give a Fuck

Dear On Top Of Old Smoky

You might try an Indian enchantment. You sneak up while she's asleep on a night when there's a full moon. Then you diddle her with a bit of deer antler, see? If that doesn't bring her around, you better blow town by morning. You could get arrested for stuff like that.

D.M.

P.S. Did she catch you with the bear? A lot of women have trouble with that.

Readers, please!—No glossies from fatties! Deer Man likes 'em slender, okay?

Deer Man Antlers

Your column is disgusting. I show it to the girls at work and we all vomit. What do you think of that?

Nausea From Way Back

Dear Swayback

A strange sexual practise, but whatever turns you on.

D.M.

Deer Man Antlers

I'm a high school boy and I'm crazy about girls. But how do I get some? When I ask them out, they just laugh. What do you think of that?

Eager For Beaver

Dear Igor

You're on the right track. Get a girl to laugh and she's halfway into bed.

D.M.

"I'm afraid of things that go hump in the night..."

Deer Man Antlers

I badger my girlfriend to let me come on her face and boobs like in the porno movies. She says it's demeaning. I say at least she doesn't have to worry about getting pregnant. She says she will go along with it if you say it's okay. Is it go? I am

Hoping For a Green Light

Dear Green Go

You may have to go to a red light area for this one. But perhaps you can compromise. First, she can smear it on your face. If it turns out that *you* like it, then next time you can smear it on hers. That way neither of you is going to get pregnant. Fair enough?

D.M.

P.S. Badger? She don't need no stinking badgers!

Deer Man Antlers

My girl says she was one of your ladies once. She says you're no big deal. And no gentleman would have jabbed her like you did with your antlers. On the whole, she says it was a subpar performance and I'm much better. She says you insisted on doing it from the rear like you would have if she were Bambi's mother. She said she appreciates an "up front" guy like me. Your way was a pain in the ass, she said, and you made hoof marks on her back. I have sent along her 8x10 glossy so you can eat your heart out because

I've Got Her Now, You Sonofabitch

Dear Up Frontal Lobotomy

What do you mean "subpar?" "On the hole," I got a hole in one! Anyway, that was early in my career. I was relatively inexperienced. You want to make a federal case out of it? But, I didn't jab her with my antlers exactly. Actually, in the heat of the encounter, they fell off and got lodged in a certain part of her behind. I felt bad, but I had to save face so I pretended it was some weird Indian rite. All in all I'd have to say it was a fairly disastrous, humbling experience. So I wouldn't let it go to your head about being better than I was. The hoof marks are my trademark—I have a stamp and ink pad like they use at the circus so people can come again. It washes off. I also use it when people want my autograph.

D.M.

Deer Man Antlers

My husband goes in for bedroom gymnastics. He seems to expect me to be double-jointed and able to levitate. Also, he wants sex constantly, and in every which place (if you get my drift). But when I see him panting hungrily for me, my heart melts. I just give him what he wants. He calls me his sainted wife. What do you think of that?

Olga Sore Butt

Dear Heartbreak Of a Sore Ass

My dear, you are indeed piling up treasure in Heaven. Would that all wives favored their husbands with such solicitude. I'm awarding you the "Croix de Deer Man" for sacrifice below and beyond the call of dirty!

D.M.

Deer Man Antlers

How do you know if a girl is interested in sex? I don't want to ask her right out. But I don't want to waste a date on her if she's not. And do they expect a fancy dinner and theater, or is a hamburger and a ride back to her place sufficient inducement? I'm not money happy, exactly, but I do expect a

Return On My Investment

Dear Money Happy Returns

You sound like the sort of guy who should just go to a prostitute. You can negotiate just what you'll be getting with the price clearly agreed upon in advance. Of course, you might also get some dread disease, which would serve you right. Sex is not a batch of laundry to be sent out. It is a beautiful experience. I usually look for the girl's nipples to stick out, her pupils to dilate, and sometimes they drool a little (but not the classy ones).

D.M.

Confidential to Eat My Bird, It's Only a Swallow—I used that line once and she obliged (for a lark). As for your suggestion, the answer is no. It takes one to blow one.

Deer Man Antlers

I belong to a social club consisting of about twenty young women who believe in saving their virginity for marriage. We have social events designed to take the "pressure" off our sexual urges so that we can keep our hymens intact for our future husbands. One of several ways we do this is to have occasional buttfucking parties. My problem? I have been so frustrated because I always have had chronic hemorrhoids. Well, a girlfriend put me on to Vitamin B-6. I started taking it and the hemorrhoids vanished. While getting it in the ass at a party last week, she came up to me, winked knowingly and said, "In the swing again, I see." I smiled back and said, "Yes, thanks to your vitamin!" Now I truly know why they call it B-6. I just thought I'd pass it on to your lady readers who may be in the same predicament.

Maybe we girls should start a company and sell the stuff. A lot of horny virgins with hemorrhoids would be grateful. We could use the slogan, "Things go bugger with B-6". Or we could call it

Humpbugger Helper

DEER MAN ANTLERS

Dear Lady Bugger

Another slogan would be, "Do everything butt!" If
you ever get a bunch of your girlfriends interested, I'd be
happy to attend one of your parties and give it a "plug."
In fact, perhaps we could hold it at the Deer Mansion.

D.M.

Deer Man Antlers

I was in the library the other evening. I was at a
secluded table by myself, around a blind corner, hoping
not to be disturbed while studying for an examination.
Well, a good-looking, very well dressed man came up
beside me. He reached over to my low cut blouse, pulling
it open just as nonchalantly as if it had been a newspa-
per and he wanted to see what was on the next page. Well,
he must have been able to see my nipples and everything.
We were in a library, so of course I didn't scream. Besides,
he was quite handsome. I suppose, (to be honest), I was
flattered when he said, "Excellent," leaving me his card
(he is an attorney). Then he walked away.
I guess he wants me to call him. Is he one of those
perverts you are always talking about, or is this perhaps
a new courtship ritual among the upper classes? One is
tempted to phone him if only not to appear déclassée. I

am proud of my breasts, the tips of which are large and chewy like pink thimbles. You know, a girl *does* like to be complimented. He definitely

Liked My Nipples

Dear Nibble Nips

There are two kinds of perverts, just as there are two kinds of magic (good magic and evil magic). There are nice, sweet, good-looking Prince Charming type perverts and demented, ugly, creepy ones. The former will show you respect and a good time, but the latter are to be avoided, unless your tastes run along very kinky lines. Yes, he was probably a pervert, but, as I say, a classy one. Give him a chance. If it doesn't work out, I'll personally recommend a nice pervert. Send an 8x10 glossy with your phone number. I may be able to fix you up.

D.M.

P.S. Speaking of refined perverts, I've written another poem! On the very subject. (It's my wonderful readers, you know, who inspire me to these heights.):

A sensitive pervert with class
Was a master at making a pass.
His line was so subtle, he
Got the girl so befuddled, she
Quite helplessly proffered her ass!

"No thanks, I'm just looking…"

Ladies! Order your Deer Man T shirt (with hoof marks on the back) today!

Deer Man Antlers

There's a quiet, mousy girl with glasses who lives on the first floor of my apartment building. I often see her looking at me with great intensity. But when I try to open up a conversation she scurries back into her apartment. I think she wants to get laid but is too embarrassed to admit it. Got any advice?

Likes Mousy Pussies

Dear Mouse Trapper

Instead of belling the cat, you want to ball the mouse, eh? Well, that's almost as hard. You have noticed, they are skittish and highly mobile. There is less risk to you, however. Worst that could happen is you'd get some mouseterious disease.

D.M.

Confidential to Love With the Pooper Stranger—You don't have to put up with that shit!

Deer Man Antlers

Antlers doesn't sound much like answers. It's a really dumb pun. I hope you're better in bed than you are with puns. I think you're probably not. What do you think of that?

Available

Dear Here's Dumb Pun On You, Kid.

Put your phone number and an 8x10 glossy where your mouth is.

D.M.

Deer Man Antlers

My husband and I go to a marriage counselor. Since our problem is we are not sexually compatible, the counselor wants us to practise screwing in his office. He leaves the room and all while we are doing it. He says he can tell by the moaning noises how we are doing. I would like him to watch since it's costing us $60.00 an hour, and I want our money's worth. He says this would be unethical. I feel this is an overnice ethical consideration since we'd get more benefit from his expertise if he got a real look at what was going on. When I asked my husband what he thought, he just shrugged and cryptically replied, "What comes around, goes down."

I tried to persuade the counselor to watch, saying that no matter how good our moaning was, it wasn't the whole "ball game." He was adamant. He did offer to hire a film maker to film us, even agreeing to rebate half the $60.00 fee, since he could sell the film as pornography. I said I would rather have *him* watch than some stranger with a camera. He said he can go see the movie. Finally, he said he would accept your decision. What do you say?

Not Into Cameraderie

Good Moaning!

Wake up and smell the coffee. This guy sounds like a phony. So he can tell from the "moaning noises" what's going on, eh? Well, would you hire a carpenter to build your house blindfolded? At $60.00 an hour? And his hiring (at a profit) a third party to do his work for him is incredible. Tell him Deer Man says if he can't take the heat, get out of the bedroom.

D.M.

Note to readers—Any couples needing expert advice on the quality of their screwing please send Deer Man an 8x10 glossy of the lady in question. Deer Man has a sliding scale of fees (no charge in the case of particularly indigent, attractive ladies—especially if he can get in on the action).

Deer Man Antlers

My girl is kind of shy. She's embarrassed to be having sex with me. When we're doing it, I have to pussyfoot around the subject, as if I'm in a fog, unaware that anyone is getting laid. I have to kind of shoot the breeze about the weather in Chicago, hog butcher to the world, stuff like that. If I mention anything about the painted women luring the farm boys, look at her funny, or even just ask, for instance, how she likes getting fucked, well, it's all over. She dumps me onto the floor and is fully dressed, sitting there watching TV as if it never happened, quicker than you can say Mrs. Robinson! I guess I shouldn't really feel that I have a problem. I should just be grateful she's willing to look the other way, pretending she's not getting laid. But I have this compulsion sort of to rub her nose in it. What do you think of that? I guess I'm just a

Shit Disturber

Dear Pussy Foot In On Little Fog Feet

Perhaps you can compromise. While you're diddling her, look down and maybe say something like, "How's the weather down there?"

D.M.

P.S. Girls aren't the only ones to be bashful. We've not had a poem for a while, so here's one about a modest fellow with refreshing old fashioned sensibilities:

An immodest and horny young lass
Balled a shy, bashful lad in tall grass
But she fucked in such wise
He averted his eyes
Lest he be eying quite rudely her ass.

Confidential to What Could I Do, She Called Me a "Flaming Faggot"?—Surely, under the extenuating circumstances of this woman's accusation, your wife will forgive and forget.

Deer Man Antlers

I've heard that in Greek mythology the gods and goddesses came down on earth to go slumming and pick up some strange stuff. Well, I would like to get picked up. I don't know how to let Zeus know I am available. I am hoping you have connections. Enclosed is an 8x10 glossy and my phone number. Please pass it on. Tell Zeus I promise to strange the stuffing out of Him. Only tell Him I'm not into kinky lightning bolts and like that. I just want to light my fire with a wrestling match

Made In Heaven

P.S. I am a virgin. This is no fish story.

Dear Virgin Sturgeon (Needs No Urgin')

Actually, I do have friends in high places. I will see what I can pull (stringwise). You will need a glossy of Zeus to recognize Him when He comes calling. So I have sent you one. Don't be put off by the resemblance to me (we are related—probably third cousins about 3,000 times removed—no doubt through another such terrestrial encounter). As for the lightning bolts, not to worry! He always takes on the limitations of a man in these earthly sojourns (so it's no use testing Him).

D.M.

Deer Man Antlers

What I have to say is for testing the waters. I've never before done anything like writing to a Deer Man. I just want to get a feel for it before committing myself to seeing you (that is, assuming you are interested). But I am enclosing a glossy and my phone number, just in case. If I find out that I want you to...well...screw me and stuff, I'll need for you to know that I am small and cute with pert little breasts featuring tumescent nipples. I'm getting kind of excited writing this. Are you getting excited as well? Maybe I don't need to actually see you...maybe this is enough...Yes, I think it is! Oh yes! Yes! Oh God, IT IS! IT IS! Was it

Good For You Too?

P.S. Do you smoke? Now's a good time!

DEER MAN ANTLERS

Dear Fuck You Too

Almost. But I need a little body contact first. Jesus! Talk about your wham bam thank you ma'am quickies! At least let me watch next time.

D.M.

Readers! Send for Deer Man's free catalog of risqué T shirts, buttons and bumper stickers! Please specify "Tasteful," "Torrid," or "Industrial Strength."

Deer Man Antlers

I can't get it up. It's very embarrassing. I want to be a stud so bad I can taste it. Women seem to go for guys with cars, so I don't take any chances (I've got five of them). Also, I put on sexy airs (strutting around wearing a padded jock strap and bragging about fictitious conquests). So I don't have so much of a problem actually getting women into bed, it's just that when it gets down to the nitty gritty, my pecker won't cooperate. Then also, the ladies laugh (I guess because they feel amused when they find out that I'm kind of small, after all), which doesn't help any. To make a short shlong story short, I don't ever really have any actual humps at all. I'm hoping you've got some good advice. I don't seem to be very good at playing

Five Car Stud

Dear Itty Bitty Nitty Gritty or Hump Free Braggart

Your problem is a common one. You need one of those implants (a splint they put inside that keeps it up). They haven't figured out how to make it ever go down, but so what? This way you won't even need to pad your jockstrap. Any eye, ear, nose, throat and privy member specialist can help you with it. Another thing you might want to consider are those condoms (SuppSafes) that hold it up. It's the same principle as support nylons that women wear, only these are extra reinforced. Guaranteed to hold any pecker perpendicular.

D.M.

Deer Man Antlers

The girls in my sorority drew straws and I lost, so I have to write and offer myself to you, naked (except for the bow) and giftwrapped! So here's my glossy, etc. But

DEER MAN ANTLERS

I'm not looking forward to it because the ones that talk about how good they are generally prove to be the worst. However, a

Deal's a Deal

Dear Nude Deal

Give me a chance. I don't talk about it because I like to. I'm naturally quiet and discreet. It's just my job to shoot my mouth off. It stirs up controversy, sells newspapers, panders to the lowest common denominator. All that good stuff. Trust me.

D.M.

Readers! Spare phrophylactics can be donated to charity, helping underprivileged children who may otherwise swell the teen pregnancy statistics. For the thrill of face to face giving, why not stop a kid in the street, then give him or her some directly? Girls, of course, won't be as familiar with them and may require a demonstration of their use. In this way you will be doing all us taxpayers a favor, who too often end up supporting these unwanted babies.

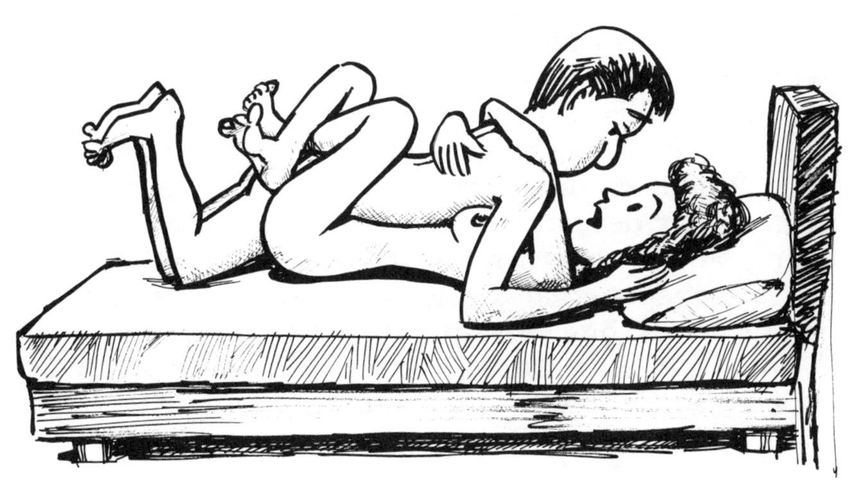

"This is a trick to get me into bed, isn't it?"

Deer Man Antlers

I hang out with a fast crowd of Polish perverts whose tastes run along unusual lines. For instance, they like their women fat. Well, I was very fat and very popular. Affectionately known as the "Polish Sausage," I was a runner up in the Miss Nude Rotund contest, so you know I'm cute, too. My problem? Well, lately I have been losing weight. I try desperately to pig out, but the pounds are falling off. My boyfriend is pissed off that other guys aren't giving me the eye anymore. When we screw, his friends accuse him of "skinny dipping" (they used to call it "doing the roly-poly"). I asked if he'd "stick" around if I got thin. He looked away and then he just said "fat chance." Sign me

Chancellor Of the Ex-chunker

Dear Runner Up, the Fat Pole

This is called the "Law of Diminishing Rotunds." You may have to hang out with a different crowd. I can assure you there are people out there who appreciate a svelte woman. Yours truly, for one. But if you are determined to be fat, you should stop blubbering and feeling sorry for yourself. Do something constructive like seeing a doctor. It's possible you have a tape worm. Boy, I thought I had heard everything!

D.M.

Deer Man Antlers

When we were first married, my husband wanted me every which way. Lately, his idea of sex has been renting a pornographic video. I wouldn't have minded that, if it got him horny. But he only wanted to watch. I'd been thinking maybe I should bring some guy home and let him watch *that*. I thought it would shake him up so I suggested it to him. He got a really weird gleam in his eye, then said in a low voice, "I can dig it." From then on, he kept bugging me to get on the stick and find someone. The other night when I came home, he had three "pals" waiting to fuck me. I figured it served him right, but he ate it up! Afterwards, one of the guys got jealous of the other two and beat them up. He also threw out my husband and we screwed a bunch more times. We are very happy now and I have ditched my husband. I don't really have a problem anymore. I was just thinking you'd like a raunchy story with a happy ending. I am now getting

Laid From End To End

DEER MAN ANTLERS

Dear Laidy

    To paraphrase George Bernard Shaw, "Those who can, doodle. Those who can't, watch (out)!" Yes, I do love raunchy stories and, yes, I'm sufficiently a romantic to enjoy a happy ending, as long as it isn't one of those "fairy" tales. Now that we're on the subject of romantic, I want to take this opportunity to answer some charges on that "score." I seem to be getting a reputation as someone who is "only interested in one thing," lacking any romance in his soul. Not true. I want to make that perfectly clear. As a matter of fact, my favorite poem in my youth was "Jenny Kissed Me" by Leigh Hunt (a contemporary of Lord Byron). I will quote it for any doubters who yet would impugn my romantic nature:

Jenny Kissed Me

Jenny kissed me when we met,
Jumping from the chair she sat in.
Time you thief who loves to get
Sweets into your sack, put that in!

Say I'm weary, say I'm sad,
Say that health and wealth have missed me.
Say I'm growing old, but add,
Jenny kissed me!

    Isn't that sweet? Of course, a hundred years plus have passed since this poem was written. It requires a modern update. Now that I've so thoroughly established my credentials as a romantic and as a poet, I feel I should do the honors:

YOUR HORNY QUESTIONS

Modern Update:

Jenny Banged Me

Jenny banged me when we met
Humping in the chair she sat in.
Lust, you slut who loves to get
Young stuff into the sack, put that in!

Say I'm horny, say I'm bad,
Say by rights they should have hanged me.
Say I've got the clap, but add,
Jenny banged me!

D.M.

Note to readers—Deer Man is straight; so all you homosexuals out there will please stop harassing him with
phone numbers and glossies, however cute. And hence-
forth a chromosome test will be required. There will be no
recurrence of the incident of Thursday evening. It was
most terrifyingly disgusting.

DEER MAN ANTLERS

Deer Man Antlers

In a foolish moment of bravado at a drunken New Year's Eve party I undid my drawers, mooning the party goers. When I did try to reassume 'em, a man grabbed at my breeches. Nor would he let me pull them back up unless he rogered me first on the spot. There was naught for it but to let him have at my wee arse for all it was exposed and ripe for swiving. I asked would he hie him to his consummation so as not to draw undue attention to what we were doing (wooing-wise). But as he was a-swiving he fell to such a grunting and hollowing like a very rhinoceros in rut that he fairly drew a crowd. And when he was done another man stepped up wanting a turn, and after him another, then another, until anon I had swived any man in the group who could rise to the occasion albeit his manliness was on view for all to see. Afterwards, I felt naught but foolishness to have attempted the mooning prank. I was so sore I could scarce walk. Indeed, I was the butt of a number of jesting references on that account. I don't recommend aught of my behaviour to your lady readers. Belike they will learn something from my experience. If it saves even one maidenhead, I'll warrant myself pleased. I am your obedient servant,

The Doxy With Her Drawers Down

Dear Once More Into the Breeches

You didn't send a glossy or your phone number. How obedient? Please forward particulars.

D.M.

"Strumpets and tea, Sir?"

DEER MAN ANTLERS

Confidential to If I Can Come Up To Your Penthouse, I'll Show You My View—Sorry, I'm on to the Fawlty Towers routine...Anyway, I don't live in a penthouse. Just the humble old Deer Mansion.

Deer Man Antlers

I do a lot of babysitting. Usually the husband takes me home afterwards. Unless he is ugly or something, I always try to seduce him in the car (on the way home I ask if he'd like to take a ride in *my* Volvo). It's sort of a challenge. I even know how many I've gotten to screw me (37). I keep track, sort of like a gunfighter putting notches on his gun. Isn't that weird? Would you believe I've never had sex except in a car? I am only 15, and am cute to the teeth (which never get in the way, honest). Enclosed is an 8x10 glossy of me and my mother, who is almost as horny as I am. She is well preserved, don't you think? A word of warning—we're so hot, we're volcanic! You run a risk of incineration. But if you think you can handle us, give us a call and for no charge, you'll get your ashes hauled

While You Wait

Dear Seething But Not Teething

Really, you are under age, my dear. But I *will* be calling your mother. Now that I think about it, in regard to the statutory rape laws, perhaps we can get off on a technicality.

D.M.

Deer Man Antlers

A girl in my high school class is really pretty and everybody says she's so horny she does it with anyone. I just figure hey, if that's true, maybe she'll do it with me. Especially since I am sexy (my mother says). I am not tall, but am well endowed. My mother says I'm "big as a child but twice as cocky." I am hoping you can give me some

Pervdog Pointers

Dear Cocky Spaniel

A guy's mother is always the best judge of these things. Ask her. If your mother says it's okay, that you are sexy enough, have her call the girl and put it to her. It's best for an older lady she can trust to ask her such a personal question. As you know, I don't charge anything for my advice. I just do it to help. So maybe you can do a little thing for me. Win or lose, could you send me a picture of this girl and her phone number?

D.M.

Deer Man Antlers

So what *is* the antler spread of a bull moose? That's right. I forgot. You're only a deer. And a namby Bambi deer at that. Perhaps you're just a dang queer deer. All this talk about women to throw your readers off your faggot tendencies, pretending that you dislike homosexuals! It's pretty obvious, and I can see through to the real you. Consequently, I've enclosed some 8x10 glossies of me kissing my pals. Care to join us? Come on, you never know 'til you try. It's maybe your last chance.

Queer Today, Gone Tomorrow

Dear Queer For a Day

Oh my. Homosexuals kissing each other. How épouvantable! Thanks for the warning. I didn't even look at the pictures. And this used to be a respectable heterosexual column...Why can't you people just leave me alone? I guess you're like so many people who want something simply because they can't have it. Thank God at least you guys don't know where I live.

D.M.

Deer Man Antlers

I always thought sex was just okay. I mean I fucked and all, whenever anyone asked, but it was never anything to write home about. It was just to have something to do. And anyway, why not? But wow! So that's what an orgasm is! I always thought of it like fairy tales or unicorns or that kind of thing. But they really *do* exist! And you don't have to be a virgin to get one. I'm just really excited and had to write. Also, I want to know if you want any, or are you all booked up? I am cute and petite. I've heard that's your favorite.

Little Obliging Lady

P.S. Enclosed is the usual glossy and phone number.

Dear LOL

It's true I like little women. But don't sell yourself short. Yours was a most unusual glossy. You know, big things come in little boxes, and I've got a big thing that would like to come in yours.

D.M.

Deer Man Antlers

This is a kid whose illusions are shattered. I'm an emotional wreck. My insides are all tied in knots. I got up in the middle of the night on Christmas Eve and what to my wondering eyes appeared but Mommy getting laid on the carpet by a man in a red suit and beard! I just want all the kids to know that their toys are tainted. They were brought by a pervert who takes advantage of people's trust in his goodness. I know.

I Saw Mommy Fucking Santa Claus

Dear Yule Tied or the Redcoats Are Coming!

It's cool. There was probably a Santa clause in your parent's marriage contract. Kids had the right idea, leaving out cookies and milk for Santa when he came. But Mommy knows what makes him come. You wouldn't send a sweet guy like Santa out on a snowy night without something to warm him up, would you?

D.M.

Deer Man Antlers

I used to have a beautiful girlfriend named Taffy, who refused to sleep with me. I couldn't make any headway either (if you get my drift). I had a lot of pull with her boss (my father), but even that didn't work. She always refused his proxy advances saying she was an old fashioned lady. What do you think of that? I had to break up with her because I didn't want to get married and I just couldn't

Finagle a Fuck

Dear Taffy Pull

It's true. Fucks are where you finagle them.

D.M.

Deer Man Antlers

When my wife and I go out partying, we both get drunk. The trouble is, I can't get it up when I'm smashed, whereas she turns into an absolute slut. It's tearing our marriage apart. I get really angry and want to punch holes in the wall or wallop the punch bowls! It's enough to turn a man to temperance. I know you can't help me really, but perhaps you can tell me why a man like me can't handle booze? And how does a woman hold *her* liquor? Sign me

> I Want To Be Up and In,
> But I'm Down and Out

Dear Temperance Tantrum

By the ears.

D.M.

Deer Man Antlers

I am a young lady who was just minding her own business in a dark alley and this weirdo/wino or (probably) pervert accosted me saying, "How do I know you won't pull a gun on me? People who hang out in dark alleys are not to be trusted." Thereupon, he put his hands all over me, feeling me up in a most shameful manner. When he was done, he apologized, saying he was feeling "frisky."

I forgot to mention that I am a student of karate. Instead of accepting his apology, I hurled him to the concrete, pinned him, and was fortunate enough to be able to have my way with him. What do you think of that? Don't tell me not to hang out in dark alleys—it's about time the men got a taste of their own medicine. It's a

Frisky Business

P.S. Somebody has to do it.

Dear Friskies Biscuits

Sounds like it's right up your alley.

D.M.

"Bang! Bang! You're Dad!"

YOUR HORNY QUESTIONS

Confidential to Uptight and Out Of Sight—That reminds me of a French folk ditty (it's a dirty ditty, as you might guess). To broaden my readers' cultural horizons, I will quote it in French:

> La bite de Papa
> Que l'on croyait perdue
> C'était Maman
> Qui l'avait dans le cul!

Translation:

> Re Father's privy member,
> Thought lost, alas!
> It was Mother
> Who had it in her ass!

Deer Man Antlers

My eighteen year old daughter shows no interest in men or sex. I bring handsome, horny men home and she won't touch them! Of course, it's not a total waste, as I make use of them myself. After all, if men can have their womanizing, why can't I have a few

Mannerisms?

Dear Miss Mannerisms

Send me your phone number and an 8x10 glossy of your daughter. Perhaps we can do some deflower arranging. Send one also of yourself in case we need a backup.

D.M.

Deer Man Antlers

I am a man of leisure, a connoisseur of the finer things in life. As one bon vivant to another, I am applying to you for advice. I have heard of a practise of the ancient Romans at their orgies. They use feathers to cause them to regurgitate their food so they can keep on eating. I have tried this, as I am keen on excess of all kinds. But is there a way I can keep my sexual desire unabated, just as the Romans kept from dulling their appetite for food? Food is nice, however it only goes so far in gratifying the body's lusts. After a few rounds with feathers and fancy cuisine, I get bored and crave actual debauchery. But if the girl is young and succulent, I quickly get excited, then, Kablooey! It's back to the feathers and food again. What do you suggest? How can I make it last? I am a

Patron Of the Tarts

Dear Pantry Waste or Feather In Your Crap

He who makes it last, makes it best. Try (during sex) to still the mind, focussing on metaphysical truths. If you can rise above the things of this world, you will not be so excited by them. For within the seed of excitement is the germ of its destruction. It's like Jesus said, "Don't let your left hand know what your right hand is doing." Of course, in this case, we are referring to a different member (the privy one). But the principle is the same.

D.M.

Readers! Tired of hearing about Robert Redford, Deer Man, and other good-looking guys getting all the girls? Want to get in on some of the action? Send for Deer Man's booklet, *How To Turn Your Bed Into a Cute Girl Trap*. It tells you how to set the trap, how to bait it, and if at first that doesn't work, how you can, with practise, become a master baiter.

Deer Man Antlers

I never get enough sex, though I have probably fifteen guys a week. It's really fun and word gets around, so I have offers coming over the phone. Still, there's always room for one more, as it were. Enclosed is an 8x10 glossy and my phone number. What do you think of that?

Horny In Hackensack

Dear Horny In the Sack

You're in luck. I'm making a rare appearance in Hackensack next week. I'll be giving a talk: "Auditioning a Pervert—the Pros and Con Artists."

Get a medical checkup. Then run, don't walk, to my hotel. No, better yet, I'll pick you up at the doctor's office (Deer Man's mommy didn't raise no dummies). I'll be in touch next week with the perpendiculars.

D.M.

Deer Man Antlers

If I visit my girl and we're in the bedroom, her mother comes around, knocking on the door. Then she asks, "Do you think that's proper?" My girl just snickers and rolls over so I can stick it in her ass. I feel sorry for her mother. I think she's jealous and has needs too. But what can I do? This girl is such hot stuff, I just can't cut her mother any slack. Besides, you know what they say about

Mother Fuckers

Dear Stick In the Mudder

Tell me. Is your girl a looker? Perhaps you would be willing to send me an 8x10 glossy and her phone number. Maybe if she's such hot stuff, she's too much for you to handle all by yourself. As for her mother, is she well preserved? Maybe we can arrange a distraction for her at a strategic moment. Perhaps if we all stick together, we can come up with something that will satisfy everyone.

D.M.

Confidential to It's Fun But It Ain't Dignified—I know. That's why I wear the antlers (to restore gravity, decorum, and that elusive je ne sais quoi to the proceedings).

Deer Man Antlers

I am tired of jerking off. I want some real stuff. If a girl gives you the eye, does that mean she'll fuck? They keep looking at me, but I'm not sure how to ask, or if I'm really cute enough. Maybe they're staring at me because I'm ugly. I am enclosing an 8x10 glossy. Do you think I'm cute? Maybe I'd have better luck as a homosexual. What do you think of that?

Possibly Latent, Definitely Horny
and Willing To Try Anything

YOUR HORNY QUESTIONS

Dear Queer Jerker

All you homosexuals out there—no more glossies, okay? Let's be friends. We can do that if you stay away. All right? Don't get me wrong. I appreciate you guys. Thanks to your strange proclivities, there's a lot more women to go around. Keep up the good work—only keep away, please.

D.M.

Deer Man Antlers

You are very big where I live. I am hoping to be able to catch the wave of your popularity and ride it for all its worth. I have a scheme to get my prodigious moustache to take the shape of deer antlers. I figure if I use wax, I should be able to get it to retain that configuration. Wouldn't that be sexy? Specifically, I'm hoping maybe I can get me some of your Deer Man groupies that way. What do you think?

Waxing Hopeful In Waynesboro

Dear Moustache Rides

Sex is not a car wash. Let's not turn my dignified image into a carnival, all right? How would you keep it

DEER MAN ANTLERS

from getting crushed and mangled when you kiss? There is nothing less sexy than drooping, mangled antlers. Unless it's sex without kissing.

D.M.

Female readers! If you would like Deer Man to be big where *you* live, send him your phone number and an 8x10 glossy of yourself.

Deer Man Antlers

Maybe you can help me. When I fuck, I feel guilty. When I don't, I feel horny. It's driving me up a tree. Don't tell me to see my clergyman. He's my husband and he won't put out. I am

On the Horns Of a Dilemma

Dear Dilemma Bovary

Best thing is to divide your day in two portions. Set aside the daylight hours to sexual pursuits, then devote the evening to your husband. That way each part of your psyche gets equal time. If you get stuck in the tree, call the fire department. They have a "Nookie Ladder" truck for rescuing horny ladies in trees. See, the firemen climb the ladder, and each has a go at you. Then, when they are done, and you are thoroughly satisfied, the last fireman carries you down in his arms, looking like a hero and smelling like a rose (or whatever perfume you use).

D.M.

Deer Man Antlers

I heard the IRS was made up of hard men but this was ridiculous! I was being audited because I claimed a deduction for having an office in my home (I'm a pleasure practitioner. Maybe you've heard of my company, *Ride Her Rents Fucks*?). I thought I might as well butter him up (it made it go in easier, too). But then he said, since it was a freebie, my home office was disqualified. He said it proved nonexclusive business use! What do you think of that?

Screwed In the Ass By the IRS

Dear Screw Loose

You trusted the IRS? Send me $5,000 and a self-addressed stamped envelope (the long kind). I'll send you the deed to the Brooklyn Bridge.

D.M.

"*Instead of a bachelor party, Dear, we decided to give <u>you</u> a surprise shower!*"

Deer Man Antlers

My girlfriend does it with candles when I'm not around, which is all right. It keeps her mellow. I mean, if it weren't for that, she'd be insatiable. She's all I can handle now. My problem is, it leaves a residue. My privy member is getting a

Waxy Yellow Buildup

Dear Mellow Yellow

Have her switch to deer antler dildoes. I'll be in the vicinity a week from Friday. I moonlight as a travelling antler salesman and will be glad to treat her to a free "Deer Manstration."

D.M.

DEER MAN ANTLERS

Deer Man Antlers

Would you impart some Indian lore to your readers? I hear they believe there is a sacred heaven that God reserves for upright members of Indian society when they die. Is there really a

Happy Humping Ground?

Dear Hump Happy

Yes. This is why Nelson Rockefeller (who was, I believe, part Cherokee) enjoyed heaven on earth. Here, freely translated into English vernacular, is some sacred verse from the word of mouth Indian tradition:

> Funny ding happened on da way
> Ta da hoorhouse.*
> War walkin' 'long horny as hell
> When I got dis here feelin'
> Like I war dead.
> An' sure 'nuff I found myself
> Ascendin' ta heaven wid
> A whole slewa gorjus girls
> What warn't wearin' no close
> An' what was all fightin' fer da chance
> Ta massage me all over.
> An' I knowed den da good Lord
> War goin' ta pervide fer me
> An' I warn't never goin' ta be
> Horny no more.

D.M.

*Whoopie Wigwam

Deer Man Antlers

I live on a ranch and I was so horny one night I couldn't sleep. I went for a walk in the moonlight and ended up sitting on the fence watching my cow and the bull who started going at her (no foreplay at all). Well, I got to thinking about my (non-existent) sex life. How does that bull get off getting off like that leaving me just sitting on the fence with nothing? You got any advice? I sure wish *I* was doing that!

Midnight Cowboy

Dear Animal Acts M.C.

Why not? It's your cow.

D.M.

Confidential to Whither Thou Goest, I Will Come—How about hither?

Deer Man Antlers

When a guy dropped me off from a date, I asked if he'd like to come in for a "stiff one." Well, I had meant a drink, but apparently he misunderstood. I went into the kitchen and bent over to search through the drawers for a swizzle stick. Before I could say "Johnny-come-lately" he said, "Try this," and he searched through *my* drawers. But his swizzle stick was more like a fizzle stick. A minute, max, and it was over. Then he said on second thought, he had to drive, so he wouldn't be needing a drink. But I certainly did. He left me

High and Dry With My Drawers Down

Dear High Ball

Fizzlesticks! This guy is no gentleman. A gentleman sticks with his lady until she's satisfied. Or at least gives her a decent shot at it. Although sometimes an indecent shot obtains better results.

D.M.

YOUR HORNY QUESTIONS

P.S. This suggests a poem which echoes the distress of ladies like yourself:

> A well preserved widow from Kent
> Had a lover whose passion fast spent
> "The young man is too quick!
> He's done ere he's thick!"
> Was the well preserved widow's lament.

Deer Man Antlers

You must know that, in order not to alarm the children, my husband and I always refer to sex as "doing the laundry." It's become such a habit that even in private, that's what we call it. Well, lately I've been feeling neglected. When I ask my husband if he wants to "do the laundry," he's been saying, "Sorry, Honey, I had a small load, so I did it by hand." What do you think of that?

Unemployed Laundress

Dear Laundered Honey or Take Me To Your Cleaners!

Something is up, and it certainly isn't your husband's pecker. Unless he's matriculating in a different curriculum (if you get my drift). If so, you face two choices (what the hell, you can do them both). One is to send me an 8x10 glossy and your phone number and the other is to develop some "pecker dildos" of your own.

D.M.

P.S. Unless of course, your husband *is* being straight with you. But I always say a bird in the bush is worth two in the hand. More, actually.

Deer Man Antlers

I spilled coffee in my lap and needed to change clothes. I was at my girlfriend's house and since we are the same size—I'm small for a man—I asked if she'd let me wear some of hers. But she got suspicious when I said I would also need a pair of her panties. Well, she threw me over for someone who wore shorts "like a man." She called me a

Crass Dresser

P.S. What do you think of that?

Dear Transvesty Of a Man

Haven't you heard of "Macho Panties?" It's for the manly transvestite—the man who wants his women *and* their clothes. If they don't get your girl back, send me her photo (preferably an 8x10 glossy—I like to keep my collection uniform) and her phone number. I'll see what I can talk her into. I care.

D.M.

Deer Man Antlers

My woman keeps nagging at me about "simultaneous orgasms." How can I get her off my back? I can never come unless she gets off first. We're out of sync. And I don't think she understands anatomy very well. Our sex life is

In the Toilet

Dear Out Of Sync and Into the Toilet

Simultaneous orgasm is not what it's cracked up to be. Two quality orgasms separated by a minute or two are much better than if you are trying to concentrate on having a good one while somebody is moaning and bellowing in your ear like a rhinoceros in rut. Keep things dignified. A stiff upper lip facilitates stiff lower stuff.

D.M.

"Invite me up to your penthouse,
and I'll show you my view!"

Readers! Send for Deer Man's tasteful video "release": *Old Fashioned Girl Meets New Fangled Fucking.*

Deer Man Antlers

I should have known better. My mother warned me about men who feign a fine concern for a maiden's heart and straightway quench the burning flame o' their lust on a girl's snatch as if 't were a candlesnuffer. The saddest part of it is that after the first snuffing, it craves more candles. It's an indignity to be sure, to be so hardly used, but now I've got a craving for it in my very belly. I should be on my knees in church, but I'm on my knees snuffing candles at both ends, as 't were. I should be at my needlepoint, but instead I'm

At Sixes and Sevens

Dear Lust Buster

When you want to try a nine, drop me a line.

D.M.

Confidential to Wants More With Feeling—Yes, it's true there's not enough sex with emotional involvement. In fact, there's not enough sex, period!

Deer Man Antlers

All my life I had kept everyone in ignorance of my homosexual nature. But last year I came out of the closet (it was a broom closet). I know that you don't like gays, but surely there's more to life than mere appearances! What about my warm heart and passionate nature? Not to mention my intelligence, exotic wit and burbling (sic) effervescence? Are you going to let a little thing like my same sex get in our way (and I assure you it is very little— you would scarcely notice it)? Won't you at least congratulate me for having the courage to come out of the closet? Now I am a

Known Pervert

YOUR HORNY QUESTIONS

Dear Exotic Twit or Savoir Fairy

Wasn't it Oscar Wilde who said, "Ignorance is an exotic fruit. Touch it, and the broom is gone!"

D.M.

Confidential to A Hard Man Is Good To Find—Mae West, young lady, Mae West!

Deer Man Antlers

My wife doesn't understand why I am too tired to fuck her when I come home from work. The problem is this women's lib. I've got several women in my office who outrank me. They all expect me to perform sexually for them or I'll get fired. I'm pretty cute and these women are insatiable. I mean we're talking coffee breaks, lunch, quickies before and after work and sometimes while they are on the phone negotiating a business deal. When I get home I just don't have anything left. My wife realizes we can't afford to risk my job, but she doesn't understand what a toll this takes on my privy member. She doesn't think it's a good excuse when I say I had a

Hard Day At the Orifice

Dear For Whom the Ball Tolls

You've got it tough. Is your wife well preserved? Send me an 8x10 glossy and her phone number. Maybe I can take up some of the slack. I care.

D.M.

Deer Man Antlers

I like to go down on my lady, but my priest says it's bad because we can't get babies that way. But I like the fishy smell down there. Especially on Friday. Got any suggestions?

Sea Food Lover

Dear Mackerel Snapper

What fishy smell? I hate fish but I love the smell of a succulent quim. In any case, put some semen in a jar in the refrigerator next time you masturbate (this will make masturbation okay too), then when you want to have at your lady's snatch, put some semen on your tongue. That way there's a theoretical possibility she could get pregnant and everybody's happy.

D.M.

Deer Man Antlers

I like to see dirty movies. My girlfriend doesn't. She even insists on doing it in the dark so I can't see it going in. Is that fair? She says she'd be stark, I'd be staring and boy would that make her mad! What do you think of that? I wouldn't stare. I just don't want to be

Kept In the Dark

Dear Dork At the Top Of the Stare

What can I say? Either get a new girlfriend or a seeing eye dog (dogs see well in the dark). Check out next letter.

D.M.

"*Give me <u>some</u> credit! I was celibate all morning!*"

Deer Man Antlers

Am I kinky? I like to have my dog watch me fuck. It's really a safety thing. This way I can pick up total strangers. My dog can sense if anybody intends to harm me and he makes short shrift of them. Am I imagining it or is my dog getting off watching me? I think he is a voyeur dog. He is always dashing about on the bed so he can get a better view of it going in. It gets me excited to see him looking all wide-eyed and sexy with his tongue hanging out. Sometimes I think I'd like to do it with my dog. There. I've said it. Am I a

Hopeless Pervert?

Dear Perv Dog or Voyeur Looking At Me Like That?

Yup.

D.M

Confidential to Oh Frabjous Lay!—What do you mean, "She burbled as she came?"

Deer Man Antlers

I told my boyfriend I would write to you about a certain sex problem we're having and he got all upset. He thinks you'll want an 8x10 glossy and my phone number. Since I'm such a knockout, he concludes that you would probably come around looking for some action. Which is fine with me because I understand you like to put it in a lady's ass. Well, my boyfriend won't do it. He doesn't want to get his prissy member dirty. What do you think of that?

Hot Buttered Buns

YOUR HORNY QUESTIONS

Dear Hot Butt

Your boyfriend is a veritable prognosticator. I *do* want your picture and phone number and if, as you say, you're such a knockout, I'll definitely be wanting some action. Tell your boyfriend not to worry. I promise not to infringe on his territory. I'll only take the part he doesn't want. Surely he won't have some small-minded dog in the manger attitude.

D.M.

Deer Man Antlers

What is a hard on? I heard you aren't a real man unless you have one. Where can I get one? I heard you can get one from your girlfriend, or was that V.D.? Is it a Valentine's Day present? I don't have a girlfriend. I guess I need to get one of those first. Can you help me? I'm pretty small, etc. but I need someone to blow my

Eunuch Horn

Dear Horn Of Plenty

You're a mess my friend. Just buy one of those blow up plastic girl dolls. They'll go for you because they are virgins and it's traditional. But they are also plenty horny and will do anything.

D.M.

Deer Man Antlers

I sent in for a personalized license plate. It said "PED XING." They must have thought I meant "Pedestrian Crossing" because they approved it (they try not to allow anything smutty). Ha! It really means, "Pederasts Kissing." I fixed their wagon! What do you think of that?

Spring Chicken

Dear Greek Turkey

How picturesque. Okay, Smutty Pants! You win. As my readers know, there isn't much that's too disgusting for Deer Man to comment on. This letter, however, takes the fruitcake.

D.M.

"Yes, 'enterprising' is one word for it, Dear..."

Deer Man Antlers

You are prejudiced against women who expect to stay decent, even after marriage. I'm sick and tired of your posturing as a romantic, counseling men to bring gifts and love tokens to their wives and girlfriends. As if that makes up for the inherent animality of their subsequent attentions. When my husband brings me flowers, I know I'll have to spend the next two days with my legs in the air!

A Prude and Proud Of It!

Dear Prude and Prejudiced

Don't you people have a vase?

D.M.

Deer Man Antlers

I went out with a girl named Marsha. We went to a drive-in movie. She had on these pants with no zipper—just a continuous velcro seam, up one leg and down the other. It only took about two seconds to get her out of them. And she wasn't even wearing panties! But then she held up a leather bag with change in it and asked if I would like to contribute to the

Marsha Dimes

P.S. What do you think of that?

Dear Zipless Fuck

You should refer her to the Consumer Sex Index. Two bit whores used to be considered cheap. Dimes?

D.M.

Deer Man Antlers

I read all your antlers, but I never heard of a problem like this one. I was getting squished in a crowd at the Tournament of Roses Parade when I accidentally got my hand caught between a girl's legs. She squirmed and I tried to get it out, but it just got wedged in deeper and deeper and finally I felt something wet and squishy. What was it? My fingers smelled funny afterwards, but I didn't wash them. I'm hoping the smell will lead me to that girl again. Or is that

Squishful Thinking?

DEER MAN ANTLERS

Dear Squishy Washy

Your hand isn't all that could get caught. You could have been arrested for assault on pooper. If she was under age, it would have been a minor offense. If you had masturbated recently and there was any residue on your hands, you could have a paternity suit on your hands as well. It's really best to wear gloves in a crowd, all things considered.

D.M.

Deer Man Antlers

Can you help me? My girlfriend and I were at a party. Well, I had a couple of beers too many and got talking about our sex life. She kept nudging me like she wanted me to shut up, but, like I said, I had a few too many. Anyway, I subtly alluded to the fact that the night before she had let me screw her in the ass. Now she's all uptight and won't let me do it anymore. Not even with Vaseline. Oh, I make overtures, send her flowers, etc. But she said after that, she's no longer willing to be my

Back Street Girl

YOUR HORNY QUESTIONS

Dear Fuck and Tell Overture

Bless me, whatever do they teach them in these schools? Backdoor girls don't grow on trees. When you get one, you should treat her with respect. Boy, you sure put your foot in your mouth! Next time use Vaseline. It will go in easier and there's less risk of hoof and mouth disease.

D.M.

Confidential to I Won't Take It Lying Down—That's right. Be inventive.

Deer Man Antlers

My mother always warned me about perverts handing out lollipops. But it was only last week that I found out what the lollipops are for. The pervert (his name is "Pops") said it made *me* taste better, too. He got it all over his face though, which made him a sticky kisser, and it was cherry flavored. What do you think of that? I had my cherry on a stick! I asked Pops if he'd come again and he said, "Toots" (that's what he calls me), "I'm

Licking Forward To It"

Dear Tootsie

Sounds like you're on a roll. "Pops," too.

D.M.

Deer Man Antlers

You probably won't print this because you don't have the guts to expose yourself to public criticism. You are a degenerate. I won't call you a pervert because you seem to take that as a compliment. Perhaps it is, since it is so much higher a station than you occupy, who are the lowest of the low. It is a proof that Armageddon is near that scum like you have achieved national prominence. Well, I'd like to see you squirming in the jaws of fate when Christ comes again, gnashing his teeth. That's all I can say now who am incoherent with righteous rage. I'm one of the meek who will

Inherit the Earth

Dear Earthy Type

God save me from the aggressive ones! I printed your letter, though it's true, I'm not into exposing myself in public (I've got to draw the line somewhere). Perhaps I *will* get punished in the end, but I believe in the mystic truth of living in the present. As one masturbater said to another, "We must seize the moment at hand, and, since we only go around once in life, grab all the disgusto we can!"

D.M.

P.S. Armageddon curious. Where in the Bible is Jesus gnashing his teeth? And how much of the Bible would be different if there were xerox machines instead of monks with funny axes to grind who did the copying over all those umpteen generations between Christ and the printing press?

Deer Man Antlers

My boss says his secretaries have to earn "brownie points." Twice a month we have to dress in brownie uniforms and sell him "girl scout nookies." If we sell him our quota, (two nookies), we get a raise, and he pays for the "box of nookies" as well. So we get money coming *and* going. I don't mind the nookies (it feels good). But now he wants us to pose naked (except for brownie berets) for

117

a "girl scout calendar" he wants to hang on his wall. I am very modest (during the nookies I got to keep my brownie dress on). I'm embarrassed for everybody who comes into his office to see me naked. I'd feel like I was getting screwed twice over. Is he being fair? I'll go with your decision. I want to be a

Good Scout

Dear Goody Two Screws

You've got to be careful with bosses. Give them an inch, and they'll take six. Tell him fair is fair. If you can have a picture of him naked on your desk, (except for a bit of bunny tail fluff on his butt) then he can post one of you in his office. Otherwise his suggestion is strictly off the wall.

D.M.

Confidential to He Only Promised To Call Me, He Didn't Say What— Guys like him are giving lechery a bad name!

Deer Man Antlers

This is an embarrassing problem for me. In high school I was voted most likely to get laid by Marilyn Monroe. But she died and nobody else seems interested. The only company of that nature I seem to have is myself, if you get my drift. I am mortified. I won't tell you my real name, but I'll tell you who I ain't—I ain't

Ben Gettinany

Dear Has Ben

Come on now. There's someone for everyone! You're just suffering from dilutions of grandeur. Stop looking for Marilyn Monroes and start looking for everyday ladies. And if that doesn't work, find someone so ugly she'd stop a train. Anything is better than a life without sex. Take it from me. Anything. God, what a scary thought!

D.M.

INVASION
OF THE
Bawdy
Snatches

Deer Man Antlers

My name is Marie (after our Sainted Lady). You publicly demean sex which should be a sacred act of ungovernable reverence between two consenting spice or better yet, put by in deference to the far greater joys of celibacy. You should be ashamed. And do you really stamp a lady's back with an inked hoof print after you've had sex with her? If that ever happened to me, I'd feel marked for life. I'm surprised you get any offers at all. I am enclosing a photo of myself. Now you can eat your heart out realizing that only one who is pure (and has consequently the strength of ten) will ever get to meet me, much less enjoy the throes of connubial bliss. While you're at it, do us all a favor and lay off the

Big Boffer Routine

Dear Boffy Saint Marie

"Consenting spice?" I don't spouse you'd care to get hitched for the weekend? No, I forgot. You're holding out for someone with the strength of ten. Mama Maria, that's gonna be one spicy "meet" ball!

To your question. Some guys give hickies. I give hoof marks. Of course, it's optional. Sometimes it's wise to be discreet (so as not to bring disharmony into the home and disrupt the sacred joys of celibacy therein). But many ladies do like it and indeed, some prefer a permanent token of remembrance. So I send them to a tattoo artist I recommend. It does pay to advertise. I am, in fact, thinking of starting a "public relations" campaign with the slogan "What sort of woman has hoof marks?" It will be on billboards and magazine layouts. Or else the caption will read "You've longed to come, Baby!" Oh well, that will have to be worked out. Something along those lines. Anyway it will feature a sexy, sophisticated lady with hoof marks stamped on her back. I'm hoping it will start a stampede. I may have to take on assistants to handle the overflow. You know, like all those Santas in the department stores. Can you picture women standing in line like kids to see Santa Claus, only they're waiting for their turn with an assistant Deer Man with antlers on his head?

D.M.

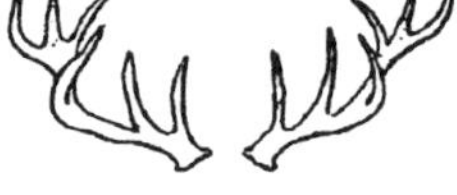

Deer Man Antlers

I run a door to door business as a nude model. It's very lucrative. I just ring doorbells at random and you'd be surprised how often it turns out that the person who lives there is either an artist, photographer or worker in a more tactile medium. But when I look at their work afterwards, I am just ashamed at the state of modern art. They must be making tons of money at it because I don't come cheap. What does that tell you about the taste of the American people? One artist coated me with fingerpaint and got undressed and we both rolled around on a bed-shaped canvas. It seemed really far out at the time, but looking at the canvas afterward, the feeling just wasn't captured. He said he was

Making a Statement

Dear State Of the Art Tart

It's like H.L. Mencken said. Nobody ever went broke underestimating the taste of the American people.

D.M.

P.S. I frequently present high class literate poetry, where appropriate, for the enjoyment of my readers. Now an accusation of literary snobbery has come to my attention. I (moi!) am faulted for ignoring the great body of folk literature which, however it may fail in technical application of the rules of grammar, etc., yet captures a feeling which renders it worthy of the attention of educated, sensitive people. In this spirit I have composed a rather rustic poem inspired by the above letter:

A loose woman had setch a good heart
'T warn't fair people called her a tart!
Jest because she posed nude fer
Artists who screwed her...
So what? She done it fer art!

Deer Man Antlers

I just learned to masturbate. Last week my older sister caught me at it. She said my wee wee had to be "grounded." She put it in her and wouldn't let it out for ten minutes. Then she made me promise to confess whenever I masturbated in the future and to face up to my punishment or I would get pimples. Can she really give me pimples? What are pimples? Is that what they call a venereal disease?

One Perplexed Kid

Dear Undersexed Kid

No, it's just your eyesight you lose from masturbating. Your sister needs a talking to, and possibly a good licking. Send me her phone number (and a photo). I care.

D.M.

Readers! Enjoy the sex act before congress repeals it!

Deer Man Antlers

In my work for the railroad, I found a sign on a railroad car that said, DO NOT HUMP. It didn't scare me. In fact, I stole it and took it home to put on my bedroom wall as a reminder of the futility of moral proscriptions. Still, it seems an odd sign for a railroad car. Can you explain? I'm stumped.

Sign Me Curious, But Not Yellow

Dear Sign Of the Times

I checked with my panel of railroad experts who said that the problem with hobos and hippies riding the trains was really getting out of hand. If they couldn't stop them from getting free rides, they did at least hope to prevent them from reproducing.

D.M.

Confidential to Do Not Go Genteel Into That Good Fuck—Rage, rage against the dying of delight? See, I'm a Dylantante, myself.

Deer Man Antlers

I guess I shouldn't complain. Some people don't have orgasms at all. When I think of all the horny children in China, it just makes my troubles seem so petty. However, for what it's worth, my problem is I can't come when I want to. I only have an orgasm with creeps I pick up off the street who are dirty and are only using me to get off. With nice guys, I just lay there asking if they intend to marry me. The thought of marriage is such a commitment, they get nervous and then ejaculate prematurely, even coming on my face by way of saying they don't think of me as marriage material. Am I too pushy? Should I just stick to the winos and creeps? Should I marry one of the winos? I just want to get married.

Old Fashioned Lady

Dear User Friendly

You could get diseases from those winos. You should be more careful. I'd come on your face too, if you mentioned marriage to me. Prematurely, I mean. Actually, some ladies I've been with *have* been pretty kinky. There was one who, (during sex!), had our wedding all planned out down to the cute deflower girl. It was strange pumping it into this little person who was going on and on and on about photographers, bakeries and dressmakers. When she got to the cute deflower girl, I shot my wad.

D.M

Deer Man Antlers

I be a hotel maid and I find this man loiterin' in one of my best rooms. In fact, beatin' his meat he was, right there before God and the bathroom. I like to died! He looks up and says with a kind of a sissy grin, "I thought you cleaned this one."

I started swingin' my duster right on his head

screamin' for him to stop and get out of my bathroom. He just keep it up yellin' "I can dig it! That's right! I can dig it!" 'Til finally he get so excited he mess up my clean floor, just missing the Jacuzzi!

Well, I sat down and cried. And he, he get himself a dirty towel from my cart and he clean it up and on his way out he apologize, sayin' he sorry. Won't never do it again. I guess he be a perv dog just like you. He was wearing antlers!

J'accuse!

Dear Jacuzzi Justice

That's pretty circumstantial evidence. These days, if I were responsible for what everybody who wore antlers did, I'd be having a lot more fun! If he was a perv dog, though, at least he was towel trained.

D.M.

Deer Man Antlers

I have a system. I accost all the pretty women I find on the street and ask them straight out, "Do you want to fuck?" I find that exactly one out of a hundred does. What do you think of that? I believe in the

Process Of Elimination

Dear Process Server

It is an interesting idea sending out an advance scout like yourself. I would be grateful for a list of your successes and their phone numbers.

D.M.

P.S. Just out of curiosity, how do you deal with the other ninety-nine?

Deer Man Antlers

The guys at the loading dock were talking about how come you're such an all fired expert about sex. Who appointed you? And what knack do *I* lack? I would like to be appointed, but I'm

Disappointed

Dear Knack Knack Joke

How did I rise to this position? It's known as the Peter Principle. As for your shortcomings, all I am able to suggest is that if you know any high class sexy women who are out of your league, send me their photos and phone numbers and I promise to ask each one I select what I've got that you obviously haven't. Send a self-addressed stamped envelope (the long kind) for the ugly truth.

D.M.

Deer Man Antlers

We drew straws in the guy bar I hang out at. We like to call it a "guy bar" instead of a gay bar (though we *are* a cheerful lot). Anyway, I drew the short straw and that means I have to write and offer myself as your slave. I'm sending the de rigeur 8x10 glossy to prove I'm a man's queer (everyone says I look like Errol Flynn in those swashbuckling roles of his). I'm also sending my phone number at the bar (we all want to talk to you). I promise to be a good slave. In fact,

Your Swish Is My Command

Dear Swishbuckler

You guys better leave me alone, or I'll have you all arrested and thrown into the briar patch.

D.M.

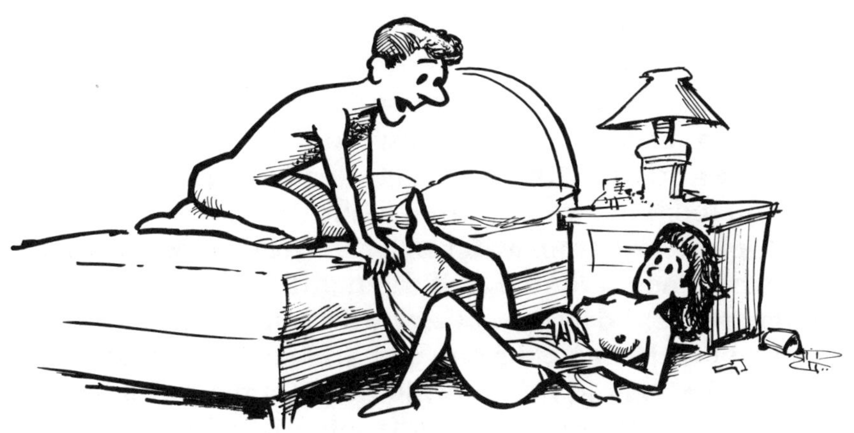

*"It's like riding a horse. It's important
that you get right back on!"*

Deer Man Antlers

As a faithful reader, I know there isn't anything too disgusting for you to pontificate on. So let me tell you about me and these two guys I go steady with. They took turns on me. One would watch while the other was doing it and get all hard from watching, then he'd be ready when his turn came. It lasted half the night that way. I came a zillion times. I'd like to get really decadent someday and go steady with a whole fraternity and stuff, except that I was so sore, I could hardly walk the next day, which was a school day. When I told my teacher I had been riding bareback, she seemed to understand. But then she suggested I try it with a saddle, holding onto the saddle horn to steady myself. She obviously doesn't know much about

Horsing Around

Dear Coming Steady or Saddle Horny

So you think that's disgusting, eh? Send me your phone number and an 8x10 glossy. If you qualify, I'll show you disgusting...As for your teacher, she may know what's up, and be trying nicely to tell you to take it easy— maybe lying on your side. If you vary the position, a different part of you gets the friction and you won't get so sore.

Speaking of that, don't get sore at my poking-fun little poem on the subject (all God's chillun' got pejorative names these days! And besides, all's fair in love and artistic expression). Here goes:

> Woozy Floozie was a whore
> Woozy Floozie was so sore...
> Woozy Floozie wasn't very choosy,
> Wooz she?

D.M

Deer Man Antlers

Since you're such an expert on Indian tradition, maybe you can explain my name. My parents only lived long enough to name me and then I got sent to a do-gooder orphanage and raised as a Caucasian. The only vestige of my heritage is my name and I've only got that to cling to. Sign me

Two Dogs Fucking

Dear Two Dog Night

When, after the birth of a new child, an Indian father steps out of the wigwam, the first thing he notices, be it a running deer or a white cloud, etc., that's what he names the child. Got it?

D. M.

Deer Man Antlers

I have a method that works well on motherly types. I thought I would pass it on to your readers. I'm on a date, see, and if the lady won't put out, I whine and carry on like a spoiled child. Before long her "no" becomes a "maybe." And If I casually let it drop that I wasn't breast fed as a baby, soon I've got her eating out of my crotch. What do you think of that?

Mother Fucker

Dear Moms Maybe

The old Oedipus Sex routine, eh? Or is it the old game, "Mother May I?" Well, it beats no sex at all by a shlong shot. You certainly have a way with imagery.

D.M.

Deer Man Antlers

I'm in love with a man who never seemed to know I existed. In a last ditch pitch for his attention, I invited him to my wedding. I wore a low cut bridal gown and as he came through the receiving line, I curtsied low so he could look down my blouse and see everything (and I mean everything!). Well, he looked and said,

"Nice Nuptials"

P.S. Since then he's calling me all the time and sending flowers. So tell your readers never to despair in love. No matter how late in the day it may be (even right up to the wedding), you still can hope to snatch the one you love!

Dear Snatch Of the Day

Thanks for an inspirational story. I hope your husband manages to find a lady to *his* liking and, through all this, manages to keep a stiff up her lips.

D.M.

Deer Man Antlers

There's a girl I know who is a nymphomaniac. I mean every time I've seen her (always in a group) she just keeps asking, "Anybody want to fuck?" I'd like to have a go round with her. She's very cute but is it sporting to proceed? It would be like

Shooting Fish In a Barrel

Dear Sports Fan

Fucks are where you find them. Enjoy. Send me an 8x10 glossy and her phone number, will you? Sounds like there's plenty to "go round."

D.M.

YOUR HORNY QUESTIONS

Deer Man Antlers

I have a different problem. I'm a guy who just can't seem to come. I feel sorry for the poor ladies I have sex with. I just go on and on all night and nothing happens. I've tried everything, even imagining I was doing it with Teri Garr. The girls are really sore, though I tell them not to take it personally. The other night I asked a girl if she had come and she replied sarcastically, "I came and went an hour ago!"

On the other hand, word gets around and I do get a lot of calls from girls who like a challenge. Still, it doesn't seem fair to them (or to me either, for the matter of that). I just can't have an orgasm.

How Come?

Dear Up and Not Coming

What can I say? You have an extreme case of postmature ejaculation. I would suggest you get a career as a porno movie actor (because of your extraordinary staying power) but you would be rather a washout in the apparently obligatory come shots. I always thought those were disgusting. Why do they have to mess up an otherwise titillating scene with a display of semen? Some things should be performed in the privacy of a lady's quim. I would like to hear from my readers how they feel about come shots in porno movies. Readers?

D.M.

DEER MAN ANTLERS

Confidential to Mortified Lady Hiding Under the Bed Who Fell Off the Mattress In the Heat Of Passion—It's like riding a horse. It's important that you get right back on.

Deer Man Antlers

People (especially you) make such a big deal out of sex. What's so special about sticking something into a hole? And it's so undignified spreading your legs and all so he can do it. When a boy finally talked me into it, I felt perfectly ridiculous! I just started laughing. It was really quite amusing. He had such a serious look on his face! He was trying so hard to keep it in while I was laughing, it just made me laugh all the harder until I was literally rolling on the floor. Finally, he popped out and came all over me. It was the funniest thing I ever saw! Actually, I take back what I said. I haven't had such a good laugh in all my life. It was fun. So now I'm ready to take on all comers.

Sucker For a Laugh

YOUR HORNY QUESTIONS

Dear Laugh It To Beaver

Just send me an 8x10 glossy and your phone number. I've always wanted to be a stand up comedian. Speaking of suckers, I've got something really hilarious to show you.

D.M.

Deer Man Antlers

I almost got laid last night. I have been trying for years and I thought I had it in the bag, but I struck out again. I'm going to write a book about my hard luck. It will be called "A Hole In the Mattress" by

Mister Entirely

Dear No Ball Prize For Literature

Send it to me (if it's raunchy, yet tasteful). I am a fancier of obskewer literary attempts. I am thinking of starting my own (per)version of the Random House Modern Library. I plan to call it "Horny Tomes."

D.M.

DEER MAN ANTLERS

Deer Man Antlers

I was getting married and I was supposed to have a bachelor party, but the stripper canceled at the last minute. The guys and I were sitting around disheartened, getting drunk. Then we decided that instead of a bachelor party, we'd give my fiancée a surprise shower (as a prenuptial prank). She was a little embarrassed to be undressed in front of all the guys but she's one game bird and can take a joke better than anyone and that's what I love about her. When she got out of the shower she said she felt so clean *nothing* could make her feel dirty for at least a few hours. So we all had a go at her. It was the best party ever! The guys saved enough on the stripper to contribute the cost of our first night's lodging for the

Horny Moon

P.S. What do you think of that?

Dear Wife Of the Party

Fuck 'em even if they *can* take a joke, I always say!

D.M.

WHOOPIE
WIGWAM

P.S. Perhaps since you find the subject so interesting, you would like to read the poem your generosity inspired me to write?:

An obliging and generous cuckold
Whose wife's fair breasts had been suckled
By an army of men
To a power of ten
Had them transported home by the truckload.

Deer Man Antlers

You're disgusting. I don't know how the police let you publicly solicit sex like you do. Isn't there a law against that? There *ought* to be a law! Perverts like you should be made to go up against the wall and pull down their pants and get some weird stuff they've got coming. And I'm just the man to do it. What do you think of that?

Avenging Stud

Dear Scavenging Stud

I told you homos to stop writing. Oh well, at least you didn't send a photo. As for the law, the cops all know that if it weren't for sex they wouldn't be here. They are grateful to anyone who keeps the ball rolling.

D.M.

Confidential to Spanky Panky—Just tell him, "Watch the fingers, buster!"

Deer Man Antlers

There's a guy on the street corner where my bus stops. He always has antlers on his head and solicits all the girls at the bus stop, asking for "spare fucks." He says he is a "pan antler." Do you have anything to do with this? If so, you should be ashamed. He isn't even handsome. But he looks so horny, the antlers are

Positively Redundant

P. S. You may be able to sweet talk naive innocent women with kinky proclivities into your bed, but how can you justify using your column for procuring them? Isn't this a breach of public trust?

Dear Breach Of Pelvic Thrust

You can't take them with you, you know. Perhaps you ought to consider the odd offer. But in any case, you shouldn't hold an idea responsible for who subscribes to it. And I've got to make a living. I should give up my lucrative column and antler sales so you don't have a dirty story to tell? Come on! As for your other question, let's just say D.M. justifies the means.

D.M.

Confidential to Shlong Days Journey Into Night—I always say, he who makes it last, makes it best, but this is ridiculous. I guess, though, it's kind of dramatic riding off into the sunset like that.

Deer Man Antlers

I'm into the spiritual aspects of fucking. I hear there's this tantric stuff where you go real slow, in and out, or do you just stay put? And the tensions build up until Kablamm! You pop off like Mount Vesuvius. Please explain. I want to use sex to

Get Higher

Dear Sex For Higher

Your true mystics are unaccountably down on this lust stuff. And we lustful guys, conversely, are not qualified to discourse on which spiritual experiences, if any, can be had along with your girl. Let me know, however, if you are ever canonized (shot from guns—like the wild oats commercials!).

D.M.

Deer Man Antlers

A cute girl I know, whenever we talk, sort of puts her hand on my crotch. No, really, she does. Is she trying to tell me something? I get all hard when this happens. Is my body trying to tell me something? Her mother (who is always with her) glares at me like I was a dog crapping on her carpet. Is she trying to tell me something? Is this what they call

Body Language?

Dear Bawdy Language

Yes, indeed. There is no mistaking any of these invitations. See, the girl and your privy member are in collusion. But both of you are on a collision course with her mother. Best idea is to get the girl in the habit of sitting on your lap. This will make her mother glare at you, but what the hell. She's doing that anyway. Then one day, when the pattern is established, have her wear a long skirt and no panties. Then you can have at her while she's in your lap and has the skirt hanging down to hide the action. Her mother may be tipped off by the rocking motion she'll have in your lap, and will perhaps glare at you. But, as I say, she's probably doing that already anyway.

D.M.

Deer Man Antlers

If a lady who sends her photograph and phone number never hears from you, surely you realize she is going to feel rejected—weighed and found not wanton enough. That's the worst result of your public solicitation of sex. I'm prone to lustful expression myself, so I don't make judgments on that "score." And you don't seem all that bad a sort, really. But have you never thought about that? Can you close your heart to the anxiety your rejection is bound to produce?

Just Wondering

YOUR HORNY QUESTIONS

Dear Wonderlust

Nobody should feel slighted not to be selected by Deer Man. I've got letters from all over the country and I'm only one man. Few are upset if they aren't chosen Miss America. Why should they take my "rejection" to heart? Obviously I don't have time for all the pretty women who write. It's the law of supply and Deer Man. Of course, I pick the ones I like best. That's one of the perquisites of my position. To tell you the truth, I've been told I have strange taste in women. Perhaps the ones I select should be the ones to be insulted.

D.M.

Deer Man Antlers

A girl I met at a singles bar came home with me. We went to bed, and she was really enjoying herself, thrashing about suitably. But she started moaning, "Freddy! Oh, Freddy!" Well, my name is John. I thought that was in terrible taste. I pointedly reminded her what my name was. She replied, "Freddy or not, here I come!" She proceeded to clutch frantically at me, making deep scratches down my back, raising welts. She didn't appear the least remorseful afterwards, and wouldn't even tell me who this famous Freddy was. What do you think of that?

Abused In Minneapolis

DEER MAN ANTLERS

Dear Abby

Lots of guys would give anything to be abused like that. However, if you're that picky, maybe you should stick to self abuse.

D.M

Readers, you're in luck! This whiner's letter has inspired a little poem which is herewith offered to help expand your cultural horizons and provide food for thought about a pressing social problem:

> In bed a girl thrashed about suitably
> But she kept a straight face, quite inscrutably
> She thought if the man knew
> How she fancied the screw,
> He would think her a whore, indubitably.

Men, why *do* you put women through this? Don't you realize you're ruining it for us all? Killing the goose that lays the golden egg? As one lady said to me recently, "I didn't mind the *fucking*, it was the *mind* fucking!" For God's sake, you guys! Let's declare a moratorium on accusing women of being whores (except in jest—mustn't take anything too seriously!) before the situation gets out of hand (or back into it) and none of us can get any!

Deer Man Antlers

You get upset about letters from gay men. Well, we're a refreshing change. We're lesbians and we don't want you at all. And it isn't just because you're a honky! Guys kissing girls! Yechh! What do you think of that?

Lesbros

Dear Les Be Friends

I don't mind girls wanting each other. It seems sort of natural. I mean *I* do, so why shouldn't they? The only harm would be if it took a really cute lady out of circulation. Mostly you women are much more masculine than I can handle so I wouldn't have chosen you anyway. I think it's nice there being someone for everybody.

D.M.

Deer Man Antlers

I've been trying for years now to scare up a girl who will go to bed with me. I just don't care anymore if she's pretty or not. Just so she's got a twat. You got any leftovers, or what?

Woman Hungry

Dear Woman Hung

What crap is this? I can't pass my women on to anyone! They go where they will. However, if I could, and if I would, it certainly wouldn't be to a creep whose only taste threshold is that she possess sex organs. My ladies are the crème de la crème. Talk about casting girls to swine!

D.M.

Readers! Send for *Nice Guys Finish Last*, Deer Man's guide to genteel sex.

Deer Man Antlers

As one pervert to another, I just want to thank you for making us respectable again. That is, if we ever were. I hear that social mores swing like a pendulum, but was there ever a time before this when a guy could solicit sex in a media publication and coddle us perverts and creeps the way you do? Boy howdy! I can hardly wait 'til it's okay to grab young girls off the streets and have at them in wild and kinky fashion! Thanks for setting the trend. You are truly the foremost apostle of pervert apologists. I await further perverted developments with

Drooling Anticipation

Dear D.A.

Usually my detractors are lacking in your subtlety of approach. My congratulations to you. If you ever decide to defect, we perverts will certainly offer you asylum. "Apostle of pervert apologists." I like that.

D.M.

Readers! Do you fancy dirty talk? Do your ears perk up at the mention of smut? Do you have strange fantasies? Anal fixations?—Me too!

"I only look like a Shirley Temple.
Without the cherry, of course!"

YOUR HORNY QUESTIONS

Deer Man Antlers

My mother told us an inspiring story of when she rode a train to Baltimore in her youth. Her train ticket said on it "Surrender to conductor upon request." Well, as she had been taught obedience, she dutifully informed the conductor that she was prepared to give in at his convenience. He told her to meet him in one of the sleeping berths about midnight. She did and just as they were entangled in a passionate embrace (to put it delicately), she remembered a sign the railroad had posted on the side of one of the freight cars which said DO NOT HUMP. Of course she was in consternation over her failure to do as she was told, violating the edict of a clearly posted sign. She squirmed, trying to free herself from the unfortunate conductor who was now quite aflame with lust and told my mother that it merely meant the freight car should not be rammed in the act of coupling with another car and did not apply to people. Not convinced, she kept resisting and the ensuing struggle was noted by everyone on the train as people all gathered round either to view the commotion, or just to see it going in and out. One elderly matron was particularly indignant. She tried to pull him off but the conductor kept clinging to my mother pointing out that he would get off when he had gotten off (and not before). Finally he declared that he, the conductor, was solely responsible for berth control. Hearing this, of course everybody went back to bed and my mother also felt that he had a point. She resubmitted herself to his advances and law and order prevailed. It's the

American Way

DEER MAN ANTLERS

Dear Ticket To Ride

What an uplifting story! Your mother, too, is hereby awarded the "Croix de Deer Man" for patriotic fervor! (So that's what those signs mean. You've taken a load off my mind!)

D.M.

Deer Man Antlers

I am the 92 pound weakling that always gets sand kicked in his face by bullies on the beach. The girls didn't like me because I'm so small and I don't have a macho attitude either. I'm also a bit effeminate. I just got tired of being turned down by girls. I figured if I couldn't lick them, I'd join them. I mean I started going to gay bars and...well, you know, they *like* little cute guys and I get picked up every time. So now I'm glad to be a

Wimpy Underpowered Pick Up

Dear Macho Do About Nothing

I told you guys to please stop writing me. This is a respectable heterosexual column. Anyway, I don't want to hear about it.

D.M.

Deer Man Antlers

I sent you my glossy and I never heard from you. I think the only thing you can get up is your antlers, and *they* are probably painted on. I think you just promote the glossies to look like a stud. The reality is that you just can't handle the responses because you are impotent. You just want us to believe you don't think we're cute enough. So, on behalf of all the ladies you've spurned, I challenge you to a fucking contest! I can take anything you can dish out. I'll fuck you under the table! I'll even throw in a five minute breather every hour during which you can substitute a broom handle.

Am I On?

Dear Amazon

I don't think you can fit under the table.

D.M.

Deer Man Antlers

Who in the hell are you to tell me how and when and who to screw? Did God single you out? I suppose St. Finger pointed his peter at you! I resent your implied superiority. Sign me

Not Sour Grapes

Dear Grape Nuts

So that's it. Implied superiority. I wondered why I wasn't liked. What does Ann Landers have that I haven't got, that is the question. Probably people have trouble feeling inferior to her. Yes, that must be it. Anyway, I like your prose. Almost poetic—"tell" and "hell," and "who" and "screw"—has a nice ring to it. And that St. Finger bit. You've got me

Eating My Heart Out

Dear Antler Eater

Want to trade? You could write the dumb straight man letters and I could pontificate about orgasms. What do you think of that?

N.S.G. (See above.)

Dear NSG

You're what's wrong with Chinese food. Why should I give up my cushy column to feed your ego? I've got my kids to feed. Your (straight man, as you put it) end of the deal, you may have noticed, is not very remunerative. As a family man, I reject your offer. And anyway, the best part about being Deer Man is the steady stream of cards, letters and 8x10 glossies with their attendant explicit invitations.

D.M.

YOUR HORNY QUESTIONS

Deer Man Antlers

So you're a family man, huh? Well, what does your wife think of your misappropriation of your female readership? But I do admire your being so straightforward (as it were) about your activities.

NSG (Again)

Dear Never Say Good-bye

Do you never get tired of writing? Don't you have better things to do? Places to be? Other columns to usurp? And who said I had a wife? Kids I meant. Boy, do I have kids! And paternity suits. And lawyers' fees. I ain't lion when I say I'm the

Father Of the Pride

Dear From Queer To Paternity

For someone who pretends to be such an expert on sex, I'm surprised you haven't heard about birth control. See, there's these little balloons you can fit over your thing and presto! No kid.

No Kidding (N. S. G.)

Dear Hot Air Balloon Rides

Thanks! I learn so much from my readers! Now I

think I understand what one of my children was singing about at my last bacchanal. He woke up in the middle of the night, came downstairs, and stood stark naked in front of God and everybody and sang this song:

> In days of old, when knights were bold,
> And rubbers weren't invented,
> They tied a sock around their cock,
> And babies were prevented!

D.M.

P.S. What's this "queer to paternity" business? You sure know how to hurt a guy!

Deer Man Antlers

Deer Man my foot! I know what D.M. stands for! You have a *dirty* mind!

Wised Up Lady

Dear Used Up Lady

Congratulations! And they said my readers were dumb.

D.M.

Confidential to Chlamydia Jane—No Deer Man at this address. No such number. No such zone. Nobody here but us chickens.

Deer Man Antlers

I want you should be sex with me. I want you should take off my clothes and lick my butt and be taking my cherry. Not talking third base. You can be having my home plate. I am very cute. I prove you with photo. I am crazy for getting fucked by the man with the deer horns. You do nothing. You just call. I take care of you. You are saying give you a chance. I say to you. I give you big time. I make all the derangements! I am a

Wild and Crazy Guy

Dear Homo Plate

I guess I'm not ready for the big time. But I have posted your photo and phone number in a laundromat in San Francisco. Sit tight and await replies. Don't say I never did anything for you guys!

D.M.

Deer Man Antlers

If you get arrested for soliciting, and go to prison, you could study hard and be known as the Deer Man of Alcatraz, a famous hornithologist! How about

Them Apples?

Deer Apples

You sure know how to scare a guy! What a thought! It doesn't take much imagination to figure out what Deer Man would be up against (as it were) in prison. Talk about your Rock and hard place!

D.M.

Deer Man Antlers

I am a cute guy, but I'm too shy to chase women, so all these queers are always bugging me, as it were. They never see me go with a woman so they figure it's open season. How can I fend off the fairies?

Faggot Me Not

Dear Fun-shy

I'm not all that cute (my charm is more in my craggy good looks) but as you may have noticed if you follow my column, I do have a similar problem. Thank God they don't know where I live. Best thing for you to do is to hang out in lesbian bars. You should be as safe there as women are in the Castro district of San Francisco. Maybe you can learn not to be shy with ladies that way. I mean, where there's no chance, there's no pressure.

D.M.

"Not today, thank you."

Confidential to I Suck On the Motion—I see you've studied *Robert's Rules Of Hors D'hoeuvres (and Other Good Things To Eat)*.

Deer Man Antlers

    I am a young woman with an unusual fantasy. I would dearly love to have it come true. I want to be ravished, then pushed naked out an open window. I want a big crowd below roaring in anticipation, possibly doing "the wave." If there's no fire escape, I'll need a net to catch me when I fall. How can I locate a guy who will do it? And what about the net? Should we alert the fire department, and perhaps tip off the press (to insure a crowd)? If the crowd is cute, maybe it can have a go at me also. Will I need to get some kind of permit? I want to be

Penetrated, Then Defenestrated

DEER MAN ANTLERS

My Dear, You Look Ravished Tonight!

I guess you want to carry the old "Throw your girlfriend out the window a kiss" routine a step further. It may be that I can put you in touch with someone who will oblige you in this matter. Send me an 8x10 glossy and your phone number and I promise to look into it. I care.

D.M.

Confidential to Blow Me Down!—Keep your pants on, sailor. You're barking up the wrong tree.

Deer Man Antlers

I've got a pet peeve about your column. Will you make up your mind? Are you pro-pervert or anti-pervert? In some antlers you are reviling them, and in some you are praising them, even calling yourself one. Are you schizophrenic? Or am I being too

Pervsnickety?

YOUR HORNY QUESTIONS

Dear Pet Perv or Schizophrenic Route

That's like asking if I'm promiscuous or anti-miscuous. First, I want to make it perfectly clear that Deer Man is a pro. Most perverts are strictly amateurs. But, as I have often said, there are two classes of perverts. There are not-nice creepy ones who have tastes that are truly bizarre, even hurtful. Then there are what I call "Prince Charming" perverts. These latter represent tasteful, old-fashioned, debauchery. They don't hurt anyone and are unfailingly courteous. They have concern for the objects of their lechery.

An example of a creepy pervert is in a letter I got recently which I did not feel was worthy of an answer. I will print it, however, to make my point:

Deer Man Antlers

Dudder day was down by da docks and then Godalmighty did I see a piece of girl! Was a little eye-talian twat what had loster mudder. She warn't hardly morn twelve year old. So I tooked her home and laider but godalmighty, her cherry was stuck in thar so far I was sore fer a week, mustabin. What do yer think of that?

Child Molester

See what I mean? Aside from the refreshing lack of hypocrisy in his sign off, this man is a complete creep. In case readers are wondering, of course I alerted the police and we rescued the unfortunate girl who is now reunited with a *very* grateful mother. Need I say more?

D.M.

Deer Man Antlers

I am a pretty young pervert (I'm fifteen). Or should I say, pervertess? But I am an early developer (translation: I've got a woman's breasts with cute, turgid nipples). I get my kicks "jaywalking" which is not as respectable as it sounds. I call it jaywalking because I am naked as a jaybird at the time. So far, I seem to get away with it. Even the cops are more interested in "jay gawking" than they are in making an arrest. One day they are going to wise up and take me in (I am primed for a romp in their back seat). Until then…You busy? Enclosed is my glossy and phone number. I meant "pretty young" both ways as you can see. When you call, if my mother answers, just tell her you are my biology tutor. But do call. I would like to make you an

Immodest Proposal

Dear Jay Bait

Damn it! You make my job hard. And that's not all. I've got enough problems using my column for sex with adults. Can you imagine where I'd end up if I publicly accepted an invitation from a fifteen year old girl? If Roman Pederaski couldn't get away with it (and he tried to be discreet), I doubt if I'd have a whole lot of luck. And anyway, I'm not sure it's right. I'll have to think about that. Long and hard.

D.M.

Confidential to Aunts In My Pants—So they be well preserved, what's the problem?

Deer Man Antlers

It's bad enough that you solicit sex in your column, but all this emphasis on 8x10 glossies perpetuates the centerfold mystique—every girl has to be perfect or forget it. Well, nobody's perfect. They do it with makeup and latex and camera angles and mirrors. Wake up to the real world. And smell the coffee! Besides, what about their inner qualities? If you can't see through this skin deep stuff you'll never be happy. I'm telling you this because you're kind of cute and I care. As you can see from my enclosed photo, I am well qualified; it's not just a case of sour grapes. But I'm warning you, my beauty is poison. I'm also enclosing my phone number, but don't call. I'm bad medicine. Sign me

Deadly Doxy Temptress

Dear DDT

Actually, what I look for in the glossies is character in their eyes. And you've got character up the wazoo.

D.M.

Deer Man Antlers

I'm a young girl who is so small and tight I can only go out with guys with dippy little privy peckers. Nobody else can get it in. Of course, my mother tells me that sex is what bad girls do and maybe I'm hung up about that and it makes me too uptight as it were to get turned on properly. What shall I do? I am tired of

Teeny Weenies

YOUR HORNY QUESTIONS

Dear Teeny Boffer

There are many excellent lubricants around you can use. And where there's a will, there's a lay. It's the old principle of the thin edge of the wedge. That's why they call them tarts (because of the wedge shaped pieces). But enough linguistics. What you need is some sex therapy. Not this cerebral bullshit in a shrink's office (for God's sake you're already small enough)! I mean on the job training. Send me an 8x10 glossy with your phone number. If you qualify (only cute sexy girls respond to this particular therapy), I will put you in touch with a member of my panel of experts.

D.M.

Deer Man Antlers

I like to rip a girl's clothes off, crawl on top, come, and get back to work. A man is measured by his work in this society. Shit, if I dawdle around the way you suggest, I don't get anything done. Any girl expects your "genteel sex" routine and I'd just stay off her altogether! I just want to

Get Off and Get On With It

DEER MAN ANTLERS

Dear Off Her She Couldn't Refuse

You didn't mention how many ladies you are able to find who like your routine. I suspect none. But that only leaves you free to get still more work done. Well, whatever turns you on.

D.M.

Deer Man Antlers

Let's cut the bullshit. I'm a no bullshit lady. I would like to fuck you. Yes, I'm a fox. Enclosed is proof (glossy-wise). You a bull? I mean, are you hung? I know you're hungry. Have to be. That's how I like 'em. Lean and hungry. Such as don't sleep at night. Got better things to do. We'll see what you've got. Oh, and I don't want any hoof marks on my back. Just bring a set of antlers to sell me. I want to have them mounted for a trophy on my bedroom wall. All right? Remember, no bullshit. Straight to business (I'm all business). And a fox. Definitely a fox.

Fox Who Fucks

P.S. I don't like bullshit. But I like a bull.

YOUR HORNY QUESTIONS

Dear Nympho Insomniac

I'm ready, willing, *and* a bull. Except now I know how the guys in the Light Brigade must have felt.

D.M.

Deer Man Antlers

I'm what you call a necrophiliac. But I can never find any corpses. What do you suggest? I don't want to hurt anyone. I just want the bodies when people are through with them. I know there is a donor program for organ transplants. Is there anything for necrophiliacs? It doesn't seem fair if there isn't. I'm getting tired of the chickens in the supermarkets.

I've even tried hanging out at funerals pretending I'm stricken with grief but some well meaning person always pulls me off the deceased before I can

Consummate the Thing

Dear Chicken Consommé

All I can suggest is that you study hard and become a medical student. Or hire prostitutes. They are trained to lie very still.

D.M.

Note to readers: On the subject of necrophilia, I know a lot of readers are appalled that I include letters like this. What can I say? There's really nowhere to draw the line. Somebody will always object to anything. First thing you know, I don't have any column left (and no women, no antler sales, the list goes on). As loyal readers, surely you don't want that. So bear with me while I occasionally coddle and advise the weirder ones among us. You've got to admit, as necrophiliacs go, this guy was pretty nice. And some people *need* them to get off. Witness the following poetic narrative:

> A young lady liked to give head
> While pretending in bed she was dead.
> She blew it one night
> When she moaned in delight—
> The necrophiliac bolted, and fled!

Deer Man Antlers

I have the singular faculty of expelling large quantities of intestinal gas. I have given the matter some thought and have concluded that perhaps with the aid of a specialized nozzle, I could concentrate the force of this wind into a column of air of sufficient power to enable me to levitate (possibly while fucking). Admitting this would be a strange fetish, I would, nevertheless, like you to consult with your panel of experts regarding the theoretical possibility of this project. Not to put on "heirs," but I am directly descended from my namesake,

Richard the Lionfarted (call me Dick)

Dear Farting Is Such Sweet Sorrow or To Air Is Human

Whew! My expert on aerodynamics has bad news. No matter how you harness it, the best you could hope for would be a series of frog-like leaps which (if you ask me) would be undignified, not at all sexy, and not conducive to a sustained fuck. Though you might invent a fun game of bleep frog.

D.M.

Confidential to I Can't Believe I Screwed the Whole Thing—Once in a while it's good to do it for the fat lady.

"By George, I think he's got it!"

YOUR HORNY QUESTIONS

Deer Man Antlers

How daring are you? I like to get laid in public. I try it often and keep track of the incidents with commemorative photos (a photographer friend with voyeuristic leanings obliges me). I have a scrap book as big as a phone directory. I put little stars on my hat (a big floppy sombreroish one—I need lots of room) for each time I've done an unnatural act with more than five interested bystanders in attendance. Are you perhaps game? It usually works best with a guy who comes fast, as you have to be ready to pull up stakes at a moment's notice (to avoid cops and would-be gang bangers). So I guess you're out, actually, since you don't believe in quick sex. Anyway, your antlers would be a giveaway and anonymity is of the essence in this type of caper. But I thought of you right away because I know you like raunchy stuff. How can I find fresh people who will do it with me? If you know anyone who's into this sort of thing, let me know. I am enclosing my phone number and some

Pictures Of an Exhibitionist

Dear Star Spangled Banger

I'll turn the photos over to my panel of experts. They have lots of connections. Or try to. And, you know,

DEER MAN ANTLERS

I don't *have* to wear the antlers. I don't usually, anyway, except when making public appearances. Though I suppose that's what you could call this. But lots of guys are wearing antlers these days. As for the speed of coming, I can come quick like a bunny when it is called for. Deer Man is versatile. It's just that it makes most women hopping mad and I don't like to make waves. Well, any port in a storm, but I prefer wacs. That olive drab drives me wild!

D.M.

Ladies! Send for Deer Man's booklet, *How To Have Orgasms Like Grandma Used To Fake!*

Deer Man Antlers

It is a pity that perverts of your persuasion are allowed to mouth off in public. Do you realize how many youngsters are probably being led astray by your filth every hour? Young girls going around Bambi-eyed in T shirts with hoofmarks on their backs? What do you think a boy who sees that will think? He'll think she's easy and he'll probably be hard at it trying to get her to sleep with him. What have you got to say for yourself?

Crusader Babbitt

Dear She's Easy and He's Hard

Sounds like a symbiotic relationship to me. Yes, it pays to advertise. Anyway, T shirts don't fuck people. People fuck people. And if fucking were outlawed, only outlaws would uphold the sacred American tradition of family life. Got you there!

D.M

Deer Man Antlers

I've got a special treat for you. No teeth. Call me and I'll show you a good time, by gum!

Juicy Fruit

Dear Tooth Fairy

I guess I said the wrong thing. I guess I've insulted you guys and now you won't leave me alone. I apologize.

I take it all back. You're a swell bunch of perverts. Let me know if there ever is anything I can do for you short of meeting you or anything like that.

D.M.

Deer Man Antlers

I always had planned to assure myself a comfortable living through marrying a man who was good and rich. Well, I've been married for several years to a wealthy man whose only interest in sex has been buttfucking. I thought he was kinky, but now it seems he was kinky like a fox. Since I'm still technically a virgin, he says he can claim our marriage was never consummated, so I won't be able to get a divorce and alimony. It will be like we were never married. He says it's called

An Analment

Dear B F'd Good and Rich

An annulment, I believe, is what he's talking about. Analment is an ointment to facilitate buttfucking (which you sorely need, I would suppose). As for your virginity, that's easily remedied. Send me an 8x10 glossy and your phone number and I'll see what I can do about it. I care.

D.M

Confidential to Sir Galahad You Ain't!—No, but I use my lance a lot.

Deer Man Antlers

You know the song, *I Cain't Say No*? Well, I cain't say yes! A guy can be plumb cute with a sure enough bulge in his breeches and "say I'm real purty and start talkin' dirty," but I just freeze up. Even though I've a hankerin' for a stiff pecker somethin' fierce, well I just put the cravin' by and turn away. When he gets to the part where my lips are like cherries and he's got to have cherries or die, well, I've got a lump in my throat as big as the bulge in his pants. I'm that moved by his plea. But I stick masochistically to my virgin ways. I know I'm not a proper pervert to act like this, but I get in the grip of this unnatural compulsion and I, well, just let it have its way with me. I am so ashamed. Please help me. Enclosed is an 8x10 glossy and of course my phone number. Perhaps you could be the prince to bring me out of this bewitched state with a kiss or whatever. I eagerly await your "antler" and any other such like stiff horny parts.

Cherry With the Fringe On Top

Dear Fringid Cherry

You need therapy. The rapist, I mean the therapist I have in mind is an authority on fringidity in women. He is, in fact, an important member of my panel of experts. You need a guide on the crooked and arduous path that leads to your true debauchery. It is not to be lightly trod by the faint of heart tart. I can see, though, that you've got the right stuff. A week at the Deer Mansion should bring you around.

D.M.

Deer Man Antlers

I'm not so fortunate as you. I'm not good looking and I haven't got enough of your famous chutzpah to even ask anyone for a date. I don't have an advice column either. So I don't get offers from women. And I can't even *buy* sex without being harassed by cops out to intimidate the "johns." Now they're enforcing zoning ordinances designed to curtail budding red light districts. They've got special cute female cops posing as prostitutes and if you solicit them, wham! A trip to the slammer. I've been trying to figure a way to know if they were cops in advance of soliciting them. Have you any suggestions?

Actually I represent a large number of "johns" who have banded together to form an association to service our peculiar needs. In reality, I only represent the literate faction of this organization but the other faction, being illiterate, has had to settle for me writing on behalf of us all. However I promised to write down the words of the illiterate faction's chief spokesman and send them along to you for your equal consideration:

> Usta be a man could git his ass
> Down ta neighborhood hoor house
> And buy a fucker sumpin fun like dat
> Fer ony a quarter.
> But now, dis goddam vice squad
> Makes it so's a man ain't hardly
> Got no choice but ta git married 'r
> Revert ta animal husbandry,
> 'R like that.

I tried to dignify his rustic complaint by rendering it in verse form. It *does* have a nice avant garde ring to it, don't you think? Anyway, we'd be appreciative if you could advise us in this hour of need.

Johns R Us

P.S. They call us "johns" because our sex life is in the toilet.

DEER MAN ANTLERS

Dear Toilet Zone

      Nice poem. Not up to mine, but damned close. Not bad for an illiterate. Now, regarding your problem, you need to have a meeting with the prostitutes so you can coordinate your response to this vicious infringement on our civil liberties. Post bulletins in all the spots they frequent and get them to come to a big meeting. Knowledge and organization is power. Remember, they need you as much as you need them. Now at this meeting, at first I thought you could decide on a secret password or phrase like in the spy movies. But the meeting will probably be infiltrated by cops. So you take advantage of one big difference between cops and the real thing. The cops are very straight. The hookers are a pretty hang loose bunch sexually. They've seen it all. They've done it all. And they'd die laughing thinking about all these straight ladies having to play prostitute for real. It's easy. You simply go up to a lady who has an air of inviting solicitation and ask if she would please show you her breasts. Then, just to weed out some unusually gung ho policewoman who has gone along with that, you then ask, "May I fondle them?" If she let's you do that, I guarantee she ain't no cop! And you get a free sample if she's a real hooker. If the cop gets mad, you just point out there's no law against asking, and freebies are still legal (que vivan los freebies!).

D.M.

YOUR HORNY QUESTIONS

Deer Man Antlers

Where can a refined lady go to get fucked in high class fashion? I am pretty and petite and get no end of offers but I fear the attraction is lust for the defilement of beauty rather than the appreciation of it. I want to get laid by a gentleman with French on his tongue. I want to be skewered by a dashing sort who quotes obscure literary (or possibly metaphysical) gems while thrusting madly in my gums (a special treat—I wear removable dentures!). Where can I find a pervert with class? I've searched everywhere!

Latter Day Lady Diogenes

Dear Lady Di

This is a trick, isn't it? It's too easy. But you don't scare me. Okay, I'll bite (since you don't). Nothing dentured, nothing gained. Send me the glossy and phone number. I want to see what you've got up your sleeve and whatever.

D.M.

Deer Man Antlers

I'll be Frank with you (not my real name). I am what you call a "queer." I just want to know why you feel it's any concern of yours where I stick my dick. I have seen your picture. You *are* cute. Actually, we "queers" use Vaseline, so it's not really painful as is commonly supposed. Once you get into it (or vice versa), I do guarantee you will evince pleasant enthusiasm. I hope you'll reconsider and give me a call. But if you want to keep to your antiquated, prejudiced view of what is, after all, the wave of the future, well, Frankly my deer,

I Don't Give a Damn

P.S. I am, of course, enclosing an 8x10 glossy so that you will know that I am cute enough.

Dear Sticky Dick or Butler Fucker

You are cute enough for all abnormal purposes. However, your freedom to stick your dick where you like ends where my asshole begins, with or without Vaseline. But I often say, I'm not altogether against you guys. If you really are the wave of the future, you will give us heterosexuals a field day with all the women you have spurned and will simultaneously solve the entire population control problem. It's just that I can't stand to see guys kissing each other. Épouvantable!

D.M.

*"I feel such a boob, Dear,
forgetting our anniversary!"*

Man Antlers

I feel really righteous when I'm getting fucked. I get tears in my eyes and all I want to say is, "God bless us everyone!"

Tiny Tush

P.S. I hear you like little butts. Enclosed is an 8x10 glossy. See, it *is* tiny, isn't it? That's a six inch dildo pickle alongside, for comparison. Give me a call. I like big ones in it!

Dear Bippie Buns

What the Dickens has gotten into you? Surely not that pickle! It's true, I like them small, but talk about too little of a good thing!

D.M.

Deer Man Antlers

My boss was giving me dictation when his wife called him on the phone. I was sitting in his lap (It's an equality thing. I'm pretty short, and this way we can see eye to eye). He was getting chewed out for not remember- ing an important occasion. I felt awkward because he was apologising profusely while adjusting my brassiere (sometimes it gets too loose). He kept saying "I feel such a boob, Dear, forgetting our anniversary." I felt sorry for him. Which of us is perfect, memory-wise? His wife reportedly doesn't understand him, which is a shame because he's such a prize. What can I do to cheer him up? He has made lewd suggestions, but I'm not really sure he's thrustworthy. Besides, I'm a virgin except for once from behind (when I was drunk) and I'm saving myself for those magic words,

"You May Now Kiss the Bride and Stuff"

P.S. I'm enclosing a glossy, etc. in case you want to get married.

Dear Booby Prize

And stuff what (as if I have to ask)? But I have to admire your employer's sense of humor. And he definitely has a clever grasp of the situation. I, too, am fondle of equality.

It's true, no one is perfect, mammary-wise, however yours come close. And yes, we could get married (perhaps from behind).

D.M.

DEER MAN ANTLERS

Confidential to Some People Have Greatness Thrust Upon Them—See next letter:

Deer Man Antlers

You probably have occasions when you've got a date and can't go. Rather than disappoint the girl (who no doubt was hot to trot), why not send an understudy in your place? I promise I am very proficient and also good-looking (enclosed is an 8x10 glossy). I'd be almost as good as the real thing. Please give me a chance. I want to

Hitch My Wagon To a Stud

Dear Understud

Emerson said, "To be great is to be misunderstud." He didn't say a thing about a mister. However, if you know any misses who would like to be great (and, consequently, understud), please have them send me an 8x10 glossy along with their phone numbers. It would be appreciated. I'll tell you what. I usually just offer them a "reindeer check," but for you I'll give second dibs as a finder's fee for any that you personally line up ("procure" is such an ugly word). Fair enough?

D.M.

P.S. I looked at your glossy, but I can't really tell if a man is good-looking. They all look plain to me. A good-looking man is an ugly woman, I always say. I wonder what they see in us, anyway. Must be our sensitivity, emotional openness and artless, unaffected nature.

Deer Man Antlers

Who do you think you are, pontificating all over the place about sex? I know more about sex in my little finger than you know in your whole damned dick. I say put your pecker where your big mouth is! You probably have a damned honky dinky privy member anyway.

Hung From the Highest Tree

Dear Outdoor Privy

Actually, I'm not into pontificating anywhere except in it's proper place, the bathroom. I'm not into that messy Marquis de Sade stuff. But I admit I'm not as big as you are if you can put it where your mouth is. Unless you're one of these contortionists. Incidentally, readers, let me know if you come across any female contortionists. I've always wanted to try one. She needn't even send me a glossy. I don't care if she's so ugly she'd stop a train. Just so I can have at her in one of those bizarre positions.

D.M.

Deer Man Antlers

I am a nine year old Chinese boy and there's a girl in my class at the *I Love To Carry Manure Up the Hill For the Commune School* who sits on my hand if I leave it out. It gets my heart beating really a lot and I feel all restless and she has this funny look in her eye. So when I try to open a conversation, I can't think straight with my hand under there. The words that come out are more like turds. What do you think of that?

Young But Hung

Dear Manure Of Speaking

I'd say she likes you. She's obviously hot stuff and a pretty savvy little lady. She won't care about what exactly you say. Even a turd to the wise is sufficient. It's like I always say. Do it for the horny children in China.

D.M.

Confidential to Blowin' In the Wind—Don't catch a cold, dear. If you want to catch a hot deer, send me your phone number and an 8x10 glossy.

Deer Man Antlers

You are always preaching about being "friends" with the women you screw. And you call yourself a pervert! Well, if you are, you're the lowest kind! You're a preacher pervert. You are a misfit. Decent folk shun you, of course. And genuine perverts (yours truly included) know a self-righteous, goody-goody pseudo-pervert when they see one. Fuck this "high class, genteel" fucking of yours! I say if you see a strumpet,

Hump It! Then Dump It!

DEER MAN ANTLERS

Dear Humpty Dumpty

     I recently heard an updated version of the famous nursery rhyme (authorship unknown):

> Humpty Dumpty sat on the wall.
> Humpty Dumpty had a great fall!
> And all the King's horses and
> All the King's men
> Humped the Queen.

D.M.

P.S. At least they had their priorities straight.

Confidential to Three Holes, No Waiting—I hate it when I have to take a number.

Deer Man Antlers

     I still seem to have sloppy sex. I try hard to be genteel, but I am no Baryshnikov in bed. When I get a whiff of my girl's snatch, I just go crazy and lose control.

Next thing I know I'm lying exhausted on the floor in a tangled heap of mattress, blanket, and girl. It's scary! The room is a shambles and my girl is staring resignedly at the wall. She must love me, I guess, to put up with this, but that only makes me feel more guilty!

Alex De Frenzy

Dear Scary Shambling

Your girlfriend is tied up in this, too. There's yin and yang to every bang. What I mean to say is, your girlfriend is going to have to take some responsibility for her own good time. Tell her it's like Ulysses and the sirens in Homer's Odyssey. She's going to have to lash you to the bed so you can't hurt yourself or anybody and that way she can have at you at her own pace. And don't be so down on yourself. (Leave that to your girlfriend, *after* you're tied up.) It's like Sandy Koufax and his "fast" ball. At first he just didn't have any control. But everone knew that if he ever got any, watch out! The rest is history.

D.M

Deer Man Antlers

I am a young lady who met a very nice pervert in a restaurant. We were all at a big table, some friends and friends of friends. Right away he started making passes, saying how much he wanted me. Well, I said, I had to leave shortly to catch a plane. He was good-looking and I gathered from the talk at the table that he was a published poet. He was kind of shy, so it really surprised me when he said (right there in front of God and everybody) that he wanted to screw me in the men's room (because there wasn't enough time to go anywhere else). Well, we went in there and I can tell you it wasn't one of your "genteel fucks." I mean it would have made a good commercial for Tidy Bowl! Imagine having to look at a dirty toilet...But it wasn't his fault. There hadn't been anywhere else to go. And, too, he apologized afterwards, promising that it would be better next time. He was a real gentleman and drove me to the airport. On the spur of the moment, he decided to buy a ticket and go with me. And he made good his promise. I had known instinctively that he would. There was a *clean* toilet on the airplane! What a relief. It was all sparkly and white (I could see my reflection in it). When we came out the stewardess made a bad joke about "flying united." But I just felt great, knowing that in spite of appearances, I could trust my intuition. What do you think of that? It was touch and go at first, but he

Passed With Flying Colors

Dear Lady With a Passed

If you can't trust a pervert, whom can you trust?

D.M.

Deer Man Antlers

I got wind of your stinking poetry and it made me turn over in my grave. I am extremely sensitive to rotten versifying. It was, in fact, one such that did me in. It was so bad it was drawing flies. This explains my posthumous classic, *I Heard a Fly Buzz When I Died.*

Emily Dickinson

Dear Ms. Dick Person

Okay, I'll admit I've not covered all the poetic bases. I Probably stinted on the onomatopoeia (that "buzz" is a good example, and I thank you for it. I'm always willing to learn from an expert. In fact, I've got a whole panel of them. But, I digress. Oh, well, while I'm digressing, let me make a modest suggestion. You could put a little more kick into that one if you changed it to *I Heard a Buzzard Fly When I Died.* Maybe you did. They were probably circling overhead, as is their wont) and personification (that's your department, anyway). But, how's this for alliteration? (Please note the Emersonian touch in the title.):

DEER MAN ANTLERS

PATIENCE

I ponder your bare butt
Jutting upwards from my bed
Like eggs still warm I still
Could hatch if I warmed
Them with my body.
But I just *did* that and
Nothing happened. Only I feel
Like a father abandoning his children,
So I decide to give it another try.

D.M.

P.S. What a guy, eh? Actually, I lied. It had gotten pretty wild! I think she dropped her nail file.

Confidential to She's a Young Thing and Cannot Leave Her Mother—So, why not make it a threesome?

*"No, I didn't tell him I'm a nymphomaniac.
He thinks he's good-looking or something..."*

Deer Man Antlers

I am at my wit's end. I'm afraid you won't take my problem seriously, but it's tearing my life apart! You see, I have a terrible visual memory and I can never remember what my husband looks like. And my sight isn't any too good, either. Consequently, he's always finding me in bed with other men I mistook for him. It always turns out that these men do resemble my husband (or at least are in the "ball" park) but this isn't good enough for him. Even though they were all innocent mistakes, it's putting a real strain on our marriage! Please don't tell me to see my clergyman. I tried that and he's practically a dead ringer for my husband.

Near Sighted Mrs. Magoo

Dear Near Mrs.

Teach your husband a secret password phrase like "I want to fuck" or some such. Be sure, however, to let me know which phrase you decide upon. I won't tell anybody and will let you know if it is a good one. And please send me an 8x10 glossy of yourself (for my scrap book of people with unusual problems). Be sure to put your return address on the envelope so the post office will be able to return it to you if they should have trouble locating me.

D.M.

Confidential to Bang! Bang! (You're Dad!)—It ain't me babe!

Deer Man Antlers

I think you are probably making a mountain out of an antler hill. I'll bet you are so small you could fuck a fruit fly and have room to spare. As for your "advice," you'd have every man be a tease. "Genteel fuck," my ass! You'd spend an hour getting a woman so horny she'd be on her knees waving her butt at you in a paroxysm of un-requited lust. Give me a man who gets it in fast like an ambulance rushing to a hospital! You pose as a friend to women, concerned for our pleasure, but you are really a sadist who makes a woman grovel and plead for sex before you deign to stick it in. And it's unnatural, what you suggest.

Nature Abhors a Vacuum

Dear Nature Of Whores

It's true—not fucking *is* an unnatural act. Speaking of fruit flies, did you know that time flies like the wind, but fruit flies like bananas? And if they like bananas, they can't be as small as you say...But I digress. As for "genteel" fucking your ass (as you suggest), send me an 8x10 glossy and your phone number and perhaps we can get together over a drink (or the kitchen sink).

D.M.

Confidential to How Kind Of You To Let Me Come—
Stop in for a "cup of kindness" any time!

YOUR HORNY QUESTIONS

Deer Man Antlers

Your answer to Bippie Balls was both rude and insulting. You are always running off at the mouth about "class" and being "genteel." Well, you are about the lowest class of pervert there is. You think because you can put on airs with your twenty dollar words and make hidden references to Shakespeare and stuff that gives you class. Well, a man with antlers on his head is inherently declassé.

High Class Pervert

Dear High Chair Pervert

You probably play with your poop.

D.M.

Deer Man Antlers

I am so grateful to you. You speak on behalf of me and connoisseurs of polite debauchery everywhere, demanding a return to old fashioned, unspoiled, tasteful smut. The pornography today has been taken over by disgusting creeps. People like myself who want honest titillation now have to choose between goody two shoes softcore pseudo-porn and really gross closeups of beaver shots, or kinky scenes tinged with sado-masochism which are also degrading to women. You are bringing back pristine, traditional lust.

The worst of it is the porno movies. What makes sex sexy is psychological interaction between two people. A girl getting laid can be very sexy, but you have to show the whole girl for that to come across. What's with these porno filmmakers? They either show only a girl's face (who is supposedly getting screwed, but is she really? It's like with the moon landing. How do we really know they were there? It all could have been rigged up on a sound stage) or an ass with a cock jamming in and out. How do we know they don't hire dozens of actresses to do the face shots and a "stunt cunt" who is the only one actually getting laid? What would be sexy is to see the whole girl, so we can see her reactions while getting fucked. Now that would be high class. And what need I say about all those come shots? Perverts like us with refined taste are getting the shaft these days. It really makes me sore to think about it but it is a comfort to know that I'm not alone. You have that truly rare quality, "misericordia"—we suffer together.

Suffering Sybarite

Dear Sybaritic Sore

It is indeed heartwarming to be appreciated. Of course, I agree with you completely. I always wondered about those moon landings. But then, I'm a traditionalist, anyway. I'm against wasting taxpayers money in space. My idea of a moon shot is a lady dropping her drawers. That's when a lunar probe is called for. And it doesn't cost the taxpayers a dime.

D.M.

Deer Man Antlers

I wrote to Dear Abby and she told me not to let my boyfriend put his pecker in me. She said if he really loved me, he would wait until we were married. So then my boyfriend wrote to you, and you said I was only interested in not going to bed with him, that I just wanted one thing (abstinence). When I wrote back to Dear Abby, she said to stick to my guns, teach him to masturbate, etc. Personally, I think you are a pervert. But you say that's okay. I am very confused and I don't know whom to believe. I surely can't please everyone. But you and my boyfriend outnumber Dear Abby two to one. Should I ask my priest for a fourth opinion? But then, if he sides with Dear Abby (as seems likely) it will be tied and I will still have to choose. And then I'm back to square one. I think I'm maybe going to become a

Nun

P.S. I didn't mail this right away and I had a dream about being a nun who couldn't stick with "none." I couldn't resist whenever anyone wanted to tamper with my vows. The mother superior got quite angry. She wouldn't even congratulate me after I had managed to be celibate the entire morning! What do you think of that?

DEER MAN ANTLERS

Dear Nun On Square One

Dear Abby's not a real deer, dear. She only uses that as a salutation. Don't listen to goody goody ladies who don't have proper antlers.

D.M.

P.S. She did have a point about the masturbation. If you fuck a man, you've gotten him off for a day. Teach him to masturbate and you've gotten him off for a lifetime. And you're right. Some of these mother superiors can be very unreasonable.

Deer Man Antlers

I am a quiet, shy, retiring, respectable pervert who would like to find some delectable lady who shares these qualities but who also is wild for weird stuff. Why do only weird people seem to have a corner on weird stuff? Loud, coarse, pushy people turn me off. But the other kind are all goody goodies, or seem to be. I should talk. I'm only a closet pervert myself. Are there any refined perverts out there? I would particularly like to find a librarian (a mousy one with glasses) who likes it in the ass. Or at least a young boy. How can I find her? If you can't tell me that, what the hell can you tell me?

Zorba the Pedigreed Pervdog

YOUR HORNY QUESTIONS

Dear Zorba the Pedigreek

I can tell you about the agony of perverts who can't answer questions like yours. But I can't turn my column into a dating service for every pervdog who writes. Believe me, I get enough flak just using it to provide for my own needs. Have you tried the personal ads? I get tons of letters from young ladies who appreciate a pervert with class. So can you.

D.M.

P.S. A young boy? You Yale students and pederasts are always thinking you can slip one by me, but I'm too sharp for you!

Deer Man Antlers

I miss that mousy girl with the big ears...What was her name? Annette Puny Cellos. I don't care if her cellos *were* puny (I'm a sucker for stringed instruments). I like flat chested women. I would be hot for guys if it weren't for their male sex equipment which renders the whole idea disgusting. I hear this Annette is married now. I am not cellos of her husband. But he better be good to her. I never could understand why she liked Spin instead of Marty. Well, I guess I've rambled on enough except now she's got that peanut butter commercial. Sticks to the roof of your mouth. I'd like to stick it to the roof of her mouth sometime. I'm so small, I don't think her husband would be cellos. So whatever happened to Marty? He didn't have any boobs either. Actually, I lied. I like guys, sex equipment and all. As long as they use butter on it first (the regular kind, not crunchy style). But I knew how you feel about gays so I tried to keep it under my hat. So you can tell Annette's husband he's off the hook. But spin Marty my way if you see him, okay? I'm writing this at the Fruity Pals Bar (we're thinking of changing the name to "Queers"—after the popular television show). All my buddies here tell me not to bother sending you my glossy because you're prejudiced. Why don't you like us gays? We are the wave of the future you know. I hear that the next decade will be called the "Gay Nineties." Have I rambled on enough, or do you want to hear the one about the travelling antler salesman who met this sailor see, and...and...the guys say you wouldn't be interested. So I guess I'll sign off. Oh, I'm going to get a sex change operation (when you ain't got nothing, you got nothing to lose) so I'll send you a glossy later, after it's legit. And I'll be changing to a woman's name, too. Watch for the knockout glossy from

Lily the Gelding

Dear Skimpy Penis Butter

I'll be on the lookout for it. Be sure to fill in your name prominently on the upper left hand return address part of the envelope.

D.M.

Deer Man Antlers

What are "honorary antlers?" I see a lot of women going around with antlers on their heads. When I point out that only male deer have antlers, they say that you said it was okay, that they were "honorary antlers." I'm a lady who'd like to wear antlers—I think it makes a nice hat and of course it tells the world I'm a game bird. But I don't want to be accused of

Horning In

Dear Hornish Game Bird

It just means that these ladies are perverts too. And you're right, it pays to advertise. It was never, incidentally, intended that wearing antlers should be a male chauvinist sexist trip. Women can be just as kinky and wild as men. And besides, it boosts antler sales. Equality is always right. But when it is profitable, it is extra right.

D.M.

3
HOLES,
No
WAITING!

Readers! Send for *Deer Man's Guide To Orgasms*— Featuring over 150 (unretouched) EKG graph lines of people certified to be actually having an orgasm.

Deer Man Antlers

I am a shy young lady who wants to be defiled by a lustful, thoroughly perverted (yet sweet) guy with antlers on his head. How did you ever decide on the antler bit? You don't have to antler that. I just am absolutely amazed. It's always been my fantasy. And now I have these constant day (and night) dreams during which I am squirming libininously under your attentions. So, enclosed is my 8x10 glossy and phone number. If my mother answers, don't mention that you plan to fuck me. She caught me once with a boy who was doing it to me from behind in a deer costume. She said she was shocked by my behavior. The woman has no sense of humor. But please call and let me know what are your

Terms Of Endeerment

DEER MAN ANTLERS

Dear Costumary Behavior or Squirms Of Endeerment

The antlers are an ancient American Indian fertility symbol (Not to worry—readers should be reassured to hear that Deer Man has now had a vasectomy). It is just part of my mystique of the tribal elder counseling his young protegées in the subtleties of their sexuality, which is, after all, such an important expression of our humanity. But enough of this bullshit. We all know that what I am really referring to antler-wise, is horniness. And Deer Man is the horniest. But he definitely is sweet. Young lady, you have hit the jackpot! And I won't breathe a word of my intentions to your mother. I wouldn't want her to be jealous in case she turns out to be well preserved.

D.M.

Deer Man Antlers

Your toilet humor is disgusting. Sex is one thing. I enjoy that myself. I am enclosing an 8x10 glossy and my phone number in hopes your solicitations in print are for real. But all this crap about poop and turds and getting your hands "in the fecal material" is just too much. I read your column to get turned on and what do I find? Confidentials to "Love with the Pooper Stranger!" I think you have an issue with your premature toilet training and it's given you an anal fixation or something. (Don't get me wrong, I enjoy it in the ass as much as the next person, so don't let my complaint put you off.) Personally, I find all this bathroom talk about as appetizing as you do all these homosexuals kissing in public. Talk about your épouvantable! I am

In a Shit Snit!

Dear Snit Wit

So you're a bugger buff? My favorite. Maybe you would like to hear my latest improvement on classic folk literature:

> Little Miss Violet
> Sat on the tiolet
> Plopping her turds away.
> Along came a spider
> Who crawled up inside her
> Dodging turds, and shouting "Olé!"

B.M.
(I mean D.M.—Sorry about that!)

Deer Man Antlers

I thought my hymen was spelled "Hi, men!" Needless to say it was too friendly to last long in this cruel world. So you're too late for my cherry. But you're

211

welcome to sloppy seconds (or thirds, or—to be honest—
"humpteenths"). Here's my glossy and phone number.

Debauch Me If You Can

P.S. I've given you a pretty good head start.

Dear Project Head Start

Yup. We've definitely got a leg up.

D.M.

Deer Man Antlers

I am looking for some strange stuff. Most men are
too tame, too bland. It's vanilla pudding, let me tell you.
How about you? I am willing to try anything. Even

Butterscotch

Dear Buggerscotch

That's certainly the way to talk. However, you had
"butter"` send me an 8x10 glossy and your phone num-
ber. I am a very busy man and don't even have time for
la crème de la crème. I am now holding out for la crème

de la crème de la crème. However, a willingness to experiment, shall we say, as is purportedly the case with you, could possibly make up for some slight deficiency in the pulchritude department.

D.M.

Deer Man Antlers

There's this snotty little slut down the hall who is draining off all the men in my apartment building, leaving me high and dry. I hang out (almost literally) in the lobby looking refined and delectable but she just sashays by with about ten men in tow. I follow from a discreet distance and see them all going into her apartment. Then I walk by her door and I can hear raucous rutting noises inside. How can a respectable lady who only wants one man at a time compete with that? Don't say to wait until she's done with one—when they are through, they stagger out, obviously rendered useless for any further fucking. It isn't fair. She's depraved, but I'm

Deprived

P.S. Sometimes I just want to throw in the towel and run off to a Chinese monastery and maybe assume a missionary position working with the horny children there.

DEER MAN ANTLERS

Dear Throw In the Tao

This is one trouble with all this new morality. It encourages a disproportionate use of sexual resources. If we could only get these really sexy women sterilized, we could solve the population explosion. It's how scientists eradicated the screw worm fly. See, all the horny men flies did their thing on laboratory-prepared sterile females, who could nonetheless accommodate innumerable males. And if you're a male screw worm fly and you've shot your wad, you're out of contention. Sound familiar?

But people aren't flies, so you shouldn't necessarily judge by appearances. Some of these guys may be able to get a second wind. And the second time is often the best. At least, it usually lasts longer. As I often say, he (or she) who makes it last, makes it best.

D.M.

Deer Man Antlers

I've got a fetish for screwing sculptures of naked ladies. At least, I've always wanted to, but there is never a real hole down there. Know what I mean? Is there an inexpensive school for stone cutters or whatever that could teach me how to drill a suitable hole? I've always wanted to screw the Venus de Milo. There's something really sexy about statues. I guess it's because they are helpless and can't run away. It drives me wild. They are at the tender mercy of a fearless outlaw pervert with a stone cutting drill. What museum is she in, anyway?

Fearless Outlaw Pervert

Dear Cheap Drills

If I told you that, I would be an accessory to statutory rape. They would probably put me in jail where I would be at the tender mercy of fearless outlaw perverts. Deer Man's mommy didn't raise no dummies!

D.M.

Confidential to Amazon Grace—That's big of you, but let's not, (and say we did), okay?

Deer Man Antlers

I like to disrupt solemn occasions like funerals by means of getting fucked. I mean right there before God and everybody. Once, at a closed casket funeral, my male friend and I snuck into the mortuary. We removed and hid the cadaver (a large, corpulent man) and climbed into the box ourselves (after drilling inconspicuous holes for air).

When the funeral was underway, people became suspicious, hearing muffled screwing noises from inside. The clergyman in charge foolishly opened the lid to the casket and I popped up (I was on top), like a jack-in-the-box and writhed and carried on, howling with abandon like a rhinoceros in rut (I'm at my best with an audience).

Several ladies fainted, the rest screamed, and the men crowded around for a better view of it going in. I gave all of them I could reach a big, wet kiss. Soon, of course, the obligatory police were pulling up with sirens blaring. Fortunately, it was just as I was coming. They tried to catch us but we had taken the precaution of coating our naked bodies with Crisco. Since they couldn't hold on to us, we escaped like greased pigs. What do you think of that? My next plan is to be at the

Inaugural Undressed

Dear Inauguration Ball

I wouldn't make a habit of doing that often. People might wise up and not open the coffin—just put you in the ground. Deer Man would hate to see that happen to anybody who can tell such delightful, raunchy stories.

D.M.

YOUR HORNY QUESTIONS

Confidential to Author Of *Toilet Flushing In America*—
Perhaps yours too will be a highly trouted commentary on
the American scene. But don't look to me for publicity.
I already get enough flak from my own anal fixations!

Deer Man Antlers

You probly never heared of my problim. I got the
hots fer my wife. Now I know that's pretty way out fer you.
But I make up fer it by doing perversions on her. That way
I can still lay claim to being a proper pervert.

What perversions, you ask? Well, we don't do no
missionary positions in Muskogee. We do it all from
behind. And I mean all. That's how I knew when my wife
got all ballooned up, that it warn't mine. So it were a fine
baby girl and I struck a deal where I wouldn't divorce her
if I could have the girl too when she come of age (Her not
really being my dotter made it okay, she said. Not incest
at all). What do you think of that? But now my "dotter"
won't put out no more 'lessn I send you her glossy and a
wide open, legs in the air invitation to partake of her boda-
ciousness. Well, I guess thar's enuf to go around. 'Lessn
you been fixed, though, you better do it from behind too.
I'll not have no pseudo dotter of mine getting prematurely
ballooned up. In Muskogee we

Do No Dotter Before Her Time

DEER MAN ANTLERS

Dear Unsnatcheral Acts

I just want to go on record that I hate having to make moral choices like this. What we have here, however, is a moot point, since you are obviously a bunch of horny Yale students making this all up (your garden variety rustic type doesn't use words like "pseudo"). But I have to hand it to you guys. You sure know how to hurt a guy.

D.M.

Deer Man Antlers

I was pure until I had dinner with one of your famous perverts—he even had antlers on his head. Well, he drooled down his shirt. When I politely pointed out how disgusting this was, he let out an unsightly belch. Then, after dinner, he had the audacity to make love to me! (He had plied me with drink, which I was forced to accept, in order to get through the evening. And besides, he had driven me there and wouldn't take me home unless I agreed to take "ball" room dancing lessons from him. We didn't get past the "Fucks trot.") I would have been mortified, but I was afraid he was a necrophiliac. I think he was. He kept muttering, "My kingdom for a hearse!" I even had to contribute to his

Lush Fund

YOUR HORNY QUESTIONS

Dear Pure as Driven Slush (Sorry, Tallulah)

That hearse bit reminds me of one of my poems. I wasn't going to show it to my readers yet, because I've not been able to decide on a final version. But maybe they can help. Here it is:

> At a wake she was solemnly dressed,
> With a dildo hid under her vest.
> Though appearing funereal,
> She was feeling venereal,
> And whacked herself off with great zest

Now, I could have written it like this:

> At a wake she was solemnly dressed,
> With a dildo hid under her vest.
> More mortar than pestal,
> She was not very vestal:
> She whacked herself off with great zest.

So, which is it going to be? Readers?

D.M.

Confidential to Speak "Friend" and Enter—That's what we need again, a password! Those were kinder, genteeler times, weren't they? Kinder gives me a lump in my throat, thinking about it (and somewhere else).

Deer Man Antlers

I want to put you on to a new perversion I have devised. See, I mill around in a crowd and when we're all jammed together, I feel up girls. They are usually too embarrassed to say anything and even if they do, they don't know who did it. Some girls like it and let you get away with whatever you want. I got my hand down one girl's panties and she squirmed and stuff (I think she came). Or else you just run up behind them in the street and they think you're going to snatch their purse, but instead, you snatch their snatch. Know what I mean? Sign me

Fast Grab Specialist

Dear Specialist Last Class

I hope you *are* putting me on! A classy perversion involves the principle of consent. Once you get that, anything goes or, (as you have noticed), comes.

D.M.

Ladies! Win a trip to the Deer Mansion! Just write (in twenty five words or less) what you would be willing to do with Deer Man (Tip: kinky is okay). Please don't forget to include your 8x10 glossy and phone number!

Deer Man Antlers

I've been nosing around and I've heard that gays are having what they call "stag parties." They all come wearing antlers and leave with multiple hoof marks on their backs. What do you think of that? Just thought I'd wise you up to the scuttlebutt.

The Shadow Nose

Dear Nosy Fan Tutte

Is nothing sacred?

D.M.

Please send

Deer Man Has the Antlers to Your Horny Questions

___copies at 11.95 each=$ ___

Shipping=$ ___

Total=$ ___

California orders:
Please add sales tax of 6% ($.72) for each book.

To ___________________________

____

____

Shipping:

___ Fourth Class:$2.00

___ First Class: $4.00

___ UPS: same as first class;UPS requires a street address.

T S Press
1226 Vine Ave.
Martinez, 94553
(415) 372-0707

Please send

Deer Man Has the Antlers to Your Horny Questions

___copies at 11.95 each=$ ___

Shipping=$ ___

Total=$ ___

California orders:
Please add sales tax of 6% ($.72) for each book.

To ___________________________

____

____

Shipping:

___ Fourth Class:$2.00

___ First Class: $4.00

___ UPS: same as first class;UPS requires a street address.

T S Press
1226 Vine Ave.
Martinez, 94553
(415) 372-0707

Please send

Deer Man Has the Antlers to Your Horny Questions

___copies at 11.95 each=$ ___

Shipping=$ ___

Total=$ ___

California orders:
Please add sales tax of 6% ($.72) for each book.

To ___________________________

____

____

Shipping:

___ Fourth Class:$2.00

___ First Class: $4.00

___ UPS: same as first class;UPS requires a street address.

T S Press
1226 Vine Ave.
Martinez, 94553
(415) 372-0707